# "GO MAKE LEARNERS"

# "GO MAKE LEARNERS"

## A NEW MODEL FOR DISCIPLESHIP IN THE CHURCH

### ROBERT BROW

*Harold Shaw Publishers*
*Wheaton, Illinois*

*All biblical quotations, unless otherwise stated, are from the Revised Standard Version.*

*Library of Congress Catalog Card Number 81-50157*

*ISBN 0-87788-134-0*

| 90 | 89 | 88 | 87 | 86 | 85 | 84 | 83 | 82 | 81 |
|----|----|----|----|----|----|----|----|----|----|
| 10 | 9  | 8  | 7  | 6  | 5  | 4  | 3  | 2  | 1  |

# Contents

## Acknowledgements

Ludwig Wittgenstein first saw through the bewitchment of language, and freed me to approach theology in a new way.

Long before I thought about them, Harry Robinson, in Little Trinity Church, Toronto, was aplying many of the principles I have written.

Rosalind Deck first believed in this book, and kept it alive through the many months before publication.

# Preface

The register of baptisms of the Church of the Holy Trinity, Karachi, in the Archdeaconry and Diocese of Lahore, states that on the 16th day of December, in the year of our Lord 1924, a child named Robert Charles Douglas, said to have been born on the 30th of August, 1924, son of David Barrington Brow, Civil Engineer, and his wife Anne Louise Charles Valentine Elisa, was baptized.

I am not clear why this happened. My father abandoned church going in his teens, and apparently never darkened church doors, apart from festive occasions such as weddings and christenings, for forty years. He was eventually converted two years before he died, partly as the result of upsetting arguments with his son in pubs, hotels, hospitals, and in the pages of numerous letters. My mother was sent to a priest to prepare for her first communion as a little girl in a Roman Catholic church in Brussels, but when she asked to go again the next Sunday she was told that she now had gained sufficient religion for her life. From then on, she shared the fierce anti-clerical feelings of my grandparents, and only very late in life began to accept her son's calling as an Anglican minister. According to C. S. Lewis's picture of heaven and hell in *The Great Divorce* I have a feeling she did finally transfer her affection from the Grey City to the Realm of the Bright Spirits, But I can't think how she submitted to the hypocrisy of having me baptized. My parents were married in a registry office, and consistently raised me with a thoroughly secular view of the world, the flesh, and the devil.

Admittedly, at the age of fifteen they gave permission for me to be prepared for confirmation by Tim Brooks, the chaplain of Stowe, my English boarding school. Perhaps they assumed that since baptism had done me no harm, confirmation might be an equally useful inoculation against the religion of the British Empire. And sure enough, although the ceremony made some impression on me and I took communion at least two or three times, I was done with all religion for the next eight years. In the army I had to go to two church parades and the wedding of a friend, but I remember refusing even to attend a carol service for conscientious reasons. I did have some discussions with an Anglo-Indian officer, Walter Ward, who belonged to the Plymouth Brethren. When he was posted to another battalion he sent me Christian tracts, which I ridiculed with great amusement, and many years later he confessed that he had finally given up on me as a possible convert to the Christian faith. Another officer, a Roman Catholic, gave me a very logical proof that if there was indeed a God who was interested in us, then we should expect him to communicate with us, and that Jesus Christ was exactly what we would look for in such a communication.

But mostly I won the arguments, and I rejoiced in persuading a fair number to abandon church, going in for the usual uninhibited life of an army officer. In October, 1947 I went to Cambridge University to study economics. I had had five easy, happy years in the Army, in return for which the government was glad to pay my fees and living expenses for another five years of study.

To my horror, right at the outset of my introduction to Cambridge, a student came to my room to persuade me to attend a meeting of the Christian Union to be held on October the 7th in the Junior Common Room of Trinity College. "I'm afraid I'm an atheist, and I have no time for Christianity" was my response. But that didn't put the fellow off. "You have come to this university to study the truth, and you ought at least to find out what the Christian faith is," he argued. I tried to encourage him to the door, protesting "Yes, yes, but I haven't got time to think about that just now." It was then that he felled me with "I reckon you are dead scared to come to a Christian meeting, aren't you?" I said I wasn't and promised to be there.

I can't remember what was said by the speaker, Norman Anderson, a law professor (who later became director of the Institute of Advanced Legal Studies in the University of London). Afterwards, over coffee in tiny cups, I argued with some of the Christian students, including David Lowe, a mathematician, and David Thomson, a physicist. I remember despising them heartily. Suddenly, I am not clear why, I bolted for my room and kneeled to speak to Jesus Christ. "If you can make anything of me, please get on with it." Next morning I was waiting outside a bookshop at nine o'clock and bought myself a Bible. I didn't even know who Matthew, Mark, Luke, and John were.

A day or two later Peter Caswell, an engineering student and the heavy-weight boxer for the university, discovered what had happened, and persuaded me to meet with him every week for an hour of basic Christian instruction. I also attended a weekly Bible study in the college. The first theological book I discovered was Bishop Nygren's *Agape and Eros,* which shook me to the core and introduced me to a completely new concept of love. Soon I was told that I had become a Christian, had been born again, and therefore had eternal life. In the warm fellowship of the Christian Union I learned, at least in terms of my head knowledge, very rapidly. I remember when Peter asked me to come to a prayer group I spent several hours composing a suitable prayer, which I had to discard when I found they all prayed "freely."

The entry into churchgoing had its problems. For two or three months it never occurred to me that one was meant to *belong* to a church. I used to attend a student service late in the evening, but I was busy yacht racing Sunday mornings. Then someone suggested, "Now you are a Christian you ought to join an Anglican, or Baptist,

or Methodist, or some established church." I think the idea
of having to choose a denomination was even more upsetting than giving up yacht racing. The first choice
seemed to be between a big mixed state church like the
Anglicans in England or a denomination of real "born-
again believers" like the Baptists or the Plymouth Brethren. During one vacation in Belgium I discussed the
claims of the Roman Catholic Church with a cousin, and
then went to meet a theology professor at Louvain University. I found that he had been converted through a
New Testament given to him at the atheistic Brussels
University, and had begun to teach justification by faith
and to recommend the study of the Scriptures in French
to his students.

Some time during my second year at university I was
persuaded by fellow students that I ought to be baptized
as a believer. A few days before the date of the next baptismal service in the Baptist church I heard Bishop
Marcus Loane of Sydney, Australia, speak at a meeting of
the Cranmer Society. He set me firmly in the direction
described in this book by convincing me that the principles of baptism in the New Testament were similar to
those governing circumcision in the Old Testament. I
decided to delay my proposed baptism by immersion, con-
cluding that I had already entered into what my infant
baptism had unknowingly signified. But that was not the
end, rather it was the beginning of questions regarding
baptism and confirmation, the constitution of the church,
the pursuit of an ideal denomination, and the nature of
the Church's mission throughout the world.

For my final year at Cambridge I moved from economics
into the extremely sceptical and critical theological
faculty of the university. I then went to train for the
Anglican ministry at Tyndale Hall, now renamed Trinity
College, Bristol, where most of the students were what I
now call "Baptists in Anglican clothing." Night after

night into the early hours of the morning we discussed the
wickedness of the church of Rome, the errors of the high
Anglo-Catholic wing of the church of England, the problems of functioning in a state church, and all the issues of
faith, apostasy, church discipline, and missionary out-
reach—themes which recur through this book.

I then went to India with an Anglican missionary society to work in the Diocese of Lucknow. I had imagined
that in my evangelistic work among Hindus and Muslims,
problems of church order would not arise. Instead, I found
myself ordained by Christopher Robinson, a godly high
church Bishop, to be the Anglican staff representative in a
theological college which was basically Wesleyan Methodist in doctrine and ethos.

In training ministers for the Indian churches I was
strongly influenced by Roland Allen's great book, *Missionary Methods: St. Paul's or Ours?* (first published in
1912), and later by the writings of Donald McGavran, who
for many years has led the church growth movement. The
ideas that churches may be trusted to find their own direction with the help of the Holy Spirit, and that we must not
prevent growth by misguided rigorism, inevitably led me
toward the discipleship model discussed in this book.

Meanwhile in language school I met, and married, a
nurse working with the Regions Beyond Missionary
Union in Raxaul hospital, on the borders of Nepal. Mollie
had been raised in Cheam Baptist Church, near London.
She did her best to become an Anglican but her spiritual
and emotional roots made this impossible. When she was
confirmed, we joked that she had become "a confirmed
Baptist." It took her eighteen years to feel at home in
Anglican services, and we undertook a long denomina-
tional pilgrimage together. None of our four children, all
born in India, was baptized in infancy. Realizing that
Mollie would bear the major responsibility for their spiritual nurture, we felt it would be best for them to be bap-

tized after expressing personal faith and commitment. During our first furlough I did a Master's degree in New Testament Greek studies under Bruce Metzger, at Princeton Theological Seminary, the stronghold of Presbyterianism, and on Sundays we attended Westerley Road Church, an extremely independent congregation.

Our second term in India was mainly devoted to interdenominational work with the Union of Evangelical Students of India. I still functioned as an Anglican minister from time to time, but I was asking more and more questions regarding the whole concept of the ordained ministry and the institutional churches. When we came to Canada we attended a Presbyterian church near our home, but I travelled and spoke in many kinds of churches while I worked as Director of the Bible and Medical Missionary Fellowship. It was then that I began to find myself in the exciting ferment of the counter-culture among young people, the theological radicalism of the sixties, and the evident importance of the charismatic movement, which was gaining strength. Gradually, some clearer ideas crystallized and were published in *The Church: An Organic Picture of its Life and Mission* (Eerdmans, 1968, English title *Twenty Century Church*, Victory Press, 1970).

I then went back to study modern linguistic philosophy at the University of Toronto for four years, and taught, part time, at York University. I became convinced that Wittgenstein's method of using language games to tackle philosophical difficulties would be important in theology. Obviously this book and most of my sermon construction and teaching has been influenced by Wittgenstein in ways that I am not even aware of. The pursuit of clarity and simplicity, the reasons for the whole atmosphere that surrounds theological terms, the importance of models and what Wittgenstein called "grammar"—all these now seem to me to supply a fresh understanding and illumina-

tion of Christian faith and practice which I never found
in traditional theology.

In 1970 our family began to attend Little Trinity Anglican church in downtown Toronto. Under Harry Robinson's leadership there had grown a surprising blend of
traditional Prayer Book worship with a freedom for individuals to do their own thing in the unity of a very diverse
body of people. For the first time Mollie felt at home in
Anglican worship, and I began to feel I might be able to
function without hypocrisy as a minister. Those were the
days of the Jesus movement among young people, and of
exciting renewal in the Roman Catholic church. Somehow
it seemed that perhaps new bottles *could* be provided for
the new wine of the Holy Spirit. I finally felt ready for
my first attempt at being rector of an Anglican parish, and
we spent four very happy years in a country parish sixty
miles east of Toronto.

During the last two years there, David Sissmore was my
associate in the work among the six churches of Cavan
and Manvers. Every Monday morning we spent time dis-
cussing our ministry and studying the Bible together.
Again and again we focused on baptism as the key to the
problems at issue, and David insisted that a book needed
to be written. The Diocese of Toronto was at that time involved in a decision to drop confirmation as a requirement
for taking communion. Gradually we moved toward a conviction that our children had a right to be with us as part
of the family of Christians at the communion table. John
Hill was active in the Doctrine and Worship Committee
and gave me much valuable criticism and suggestions as I
began to write.

The first draft was completed just before I rejoined
Harry Robinson as his associate at Little Trinity, where
Mollie and I had finally felt so much at home five years
before. As I welcomed further criticism, a complete rewriting of most of the chapters seemed necessary. Roger

Beckwith of Latimer House, Oxford, conveyed valuable encouragement and made practical suggestions. Many changes occurred as Harry and I discussed specific pastoral problems in the parish. He had been using a similar model of church life for twelve years, and now the book and the preaching connected with it sharpened the radical nature of the ideas at issue.

One of my difficulties was that when I asked for reactions to the proposed discipleship model of the church there was a surprising amount of hostility. I had hoped for reasoned criticism from the Scriptures, but most of what I heard was, "This is not what we believe: Why do you want to rock the boat?" As I realized how upsetting the ideas were to so many, I had to fight my own doubts. I kept reading and rereading my Greek New Testament, studying every verse that seemed relevant, to check the validity of the model. More and more its elegance, practicality, and clarifying power gripped me. If I was wrong, somebody would have to come up with a better model. Meanwhile I found great joy and freedom in using the model when speaking to new Christians, explaining baptism and baptizing, and in the context of many pastoral problems.

Meanwhile the huge changes in the Roman Catholic church and the waves of renewal rippling out from the charismatic movement encouraged me to feel that perhaps, before our own eyes, a great reformation of the doctrine of the church was taking place. Perhaps a new model, even by means of adverse reaction against it, might help us to think through and understand how Jesus Christ is building his Church.

For the past two years I have been Rector of St. James, a downtown parish church next door to Queen's University in Kingston. From the beginning I was able to outline my purpose and style of church life according to the model set out in this book. The invitation card which was given to students in the registration lines explained that in our church, "located right on campus at Barrie and Union Streets, we welcome learners, doubters, and those who wonder whether life has any meaning at all." I don't suppose that at first sight, a Sunday morning congregation of two hundred at the main service would look much different from many other typical Anglican churches in Canada. I suppose the difference lies in myself. For the first time in my twenty-five years as an ordained minister I can feel confident in explaining exactly what I am trying to do in relation to the life and teaching of Jesus Christ and the early apostolic churches that mushroomed after his death and resurrection.

In writing this book it seemed best to state clearly the Anglican context of my ministry. The reader can make some allowances for my terminology and bias. Hopefully the arguments from Scripture will prove useful to members of other denominations in considering the discipleship model which I have proposed. Christians of all traditions should be warned that many Anglicans would disagree with my presentation, but of course there would be no point in presenting something about which everybody agrees already! The book is deliberately controversial. I hope it will at least lift the discussion of baptism out of the present confusion and into a new framework.

# Church
# Models

# 1

THE WORD "MODEL" SUGGESTS something more than a two-dimensional, flat diagram. Models are used to represent exterior form, such as model planes or cars, but they can also be made to exhibit internal systems such as those of the human body. In the natural sciences, models are teaching aids but they may also serve to suggest new directions for advanced research. For example, the dis--covery of the double helix model for the DNA molecule by Watson and Crick triggered major developments in modern biochemistry and genetics.[1]

In *The Structure of Scientific Revolutions,* Thomas S. Kuhn has used the term "paradigm" to describe a way of "seeing the world and of practicing science in it."[2] I would like my use of the word "model" to include not only the functions of Kuhn's "paradigms," but also the moral fac-

tors which science excludes from its purview. If this book
succeeds it will provide an illustration of the importance
of theological models both for Biblical study and for the
practical life of a local church.[3]

My hope is to demonstrate a discipleship model of the
church. As an Anglican minister, my church model affects
the way I baptize, welcome people to Communion, lead
worship, and expect the church to grow. In preaching and
teaching I find that my model flavors all the words that
Christians use, including words such as *faith, repentance,
church, new birth,* even the word *Christian.* One result of
this is that those who attend St. James' Church, (or read
this book) with another model of the church in mind, may
find my terminology strange, if not upsetting. Each model
of the church will mark off believers, or the Christian
community, or church members, in a different way which
will affect the practice of baptism and admission to Holy
Communion.

What then do I mean by a model of the church? The
philosopher Wittgenstein commented on the difficulty of
giving a clear-cut definition of "a game."[4] And like games,
models must be looked at, and preferably be engaged in,
to be understood. After you have played a diversity of
games such as field sports, card games, and children's
games, you come to know more or less what a game is. So
it is with models in physics, biology, economics, sociology,
and with what I call church models. As you grasp one
model of church life, experience it in practice, and compare it with others, you will learn how the model works
and how it differs from others. Its use defines it. Every
theological model is, to some degree, a caricature, something far less than the whole truth, yet it may be effective
enough to unmask inconsistencies, and to evoke responses
such as anger, scorn, or the desire to act according to the
model adopted. As long as we realize the purpose of the
model or caricature, it can help us to see clearly what we

must do, how we must change, and the moral implications of our behavior. Here, for example, are some quick caricature models of the church:

*The Probationary model* holds that baptism is appropriate only for people who have seriously considered the claims of Jesus, have understood the principles of the Kingdom of God, and have *proved* their sincerity and commitment over a period of time. Candidates for baptism are therefore enrolled as catechumens at the beginning of a probationary period of several weeks. At the end of the probationary period, the candidate's baptism is a sign or seal that he had understood the foundational principles of the Christian faith, is now making a clean break with the past, and intends to live hereafter as a soldier of Jesus Christ.[5] Since babies can neither understand, nor make, such a commitment, it usually follows that they are not baptized.

*The Cleansing model* is based on the belief that children come into the world already depraved and "contaminated" by original sin. Baptism in the name of the Trinity washes away all their sin.[6] After baptism the heart is in a state of innocency until deliberate sin occurs to defile it. Sin subsequent to baptism needs to be removed by the sacrament of penance. When sin is confessed to a properly ordained priest in the apostolic succession he can give absolution, which removes the sin stain. At death, unconfessed and uncorrected sin must be purged away in purgatory. Faith is therefore defined as a belief that membership in the true church is God's means of cleansing and salvation, and that includes submission to the ministrations of its priesthood. People who have faith in this sense are Christians.

*The Judgment model* posits that God is a Judge who keeps account of our good and bad deeds. On the day of judgment we are sent to hell or heaven depending on our performance. The church exists to tell us what is good and bad, and to encourage us to avoid sin and perform the good works necessary for our salvation. Baptism enrolls us in the Christian church, but it is those who sincerely try to do good and avoid evil who are Christians.

*The Baptist model* holds that all of us deserve to go to hell because of original sin. Sin can be forgiven only upon our decision to accept Jesus Christ as personal Savior. If we admit our sin, believe he died for us, and accept him as Savior, we are saved from our sins and born again. Baptism is the sign that we have done this and so have become Christians. Only adults can make such a crucial decision, therefore babies should not be baptized.

*The Liberation model* understands the church to be a force that motivates us in the direction of social justice. Our present economic and social structures make justice impossible, and without justice there can be no freedom and therefore no love. The task of Christians is to build the kingdom of God by denouncing injustice, and by organizing themselves and others to overthrow the existing structures, by means of violence if necessary, and so bring in freedom for a better world where love can flourish. Baptism commits us to such a struggle, which we share with all others who care about justice and freedom.

It is to be hoped that no responsible theologian would subscribe to any of these caricature models without many qualifications. But the very fact that such caricatures exist suggests that the models they represent are recognizable. We all know Christians whose beliefs follow one or other of these paths. I suspect that most ordinary church members have been taught to view themselves in relation to their church in terms of some such simple model. To theologians the caricatures may seem gross, but the fact is that such caricatures motivate action, and provide a framework for persuading others to function as the model requires. Once adopted, the model in some sense grips and molds us.

Corresponding to each model of the church there is a

community of adherents who live by the set of traditions that the model requires. The tradition of each model is developed and expressed in popular books, magazines, Sunday School materials, in worship, in preaching, and in a host of unstated ways by the behavior, body language, and accepted norms of ministers and laymen in church and in social and family situations. The traditions connected with a particular religious model correspond to what Kuhn called "normal science."[7]

I propose to set out a discipleship model of the church which we could caricature as follows:

*The Discipleship model* holds that Jesus imparted his teaching to disciples. Disciples were enrolled by baptism. Before leaving his disciples, Jesus told his chosen leaders to go into all the world and enroll other disciples from all nations by baptizing them. The baptized were to be taught all that Jesus had imparted to his disciples. In place of his personal presence among them, Jesus sent the Holy Spirit to superintend, direct, and apply his teaching among the baptized. The definition of a Christian is therefore a learner, a disciple under instruction by the Holy Spirit. A local church consists of the group of disciples gathered for teaching by the Holy Spirit in that place.

As I proceed, this caricature will be developed, given depth and inner structure. The first objective is to picture this model, in contrast to other models, as a possible form of church life by showing that the Discipleship model fits much of the New Testament evidence, is a practical way to picture the life of a parish, and dissolves many of the bothersome problems of other models. This does not prove that the discipleship model is the correct or ultimate model. *It merely proposes one possible way of picturing the Biblical data.*

How then do we know when a model is correct? As Kuhn shows, this is a wrong formulation of the question.[8] What we need to ask is, which model solves the most problems?

It is on this basis that we should decide to use one model in preference to others. If a large number of church congregations begin to look at their work in terms of the discipleship model, obviously there will be revolutionary changes in the way Christians view themselves, and in the way others, in the world, view them. Whether or not that happens, this book will be worthwhile if it helps parish ministers and thinking members of their congregations to clarify the model they intend to use in the work of Jesus Christ.

In the discussions of baptism and Christian initiation over the past few years there have been scholarly arguments for many different models. Baptismal regeneration has been opposed by those who argue salvation by faith alone. Infant baptism has been widely attacked by those who are convinced that the Bible teaches "believers' " baptism. Some have recommended a more of less lengthy catechumenate. Many ministers who practice infant baptism have become rigorous in rejecting parents who do not believe or behave or otherwise shape up. It should be obvious that radically new thinking about baptism is needed to move us beyond the present impasse.[9]

**Questions for Study and Discussion**
1  Try to identify at least one active Christian, whom you know personally, whose belief and behavior fits each of the models described in the Introduction. Next time you meet him or her, check your impression by friendly questioning (the purpose is not to win arguments, but to understand the viewpoints of others).
2  Attempt to identify the models used by some of the churches of various denominations in your area. Later you may be able to correct your caricatures by asking their members how they view themselves.
3  Does your own local church have a clear model that explains its work? Describe it.
4  Are there strong-minded individuals in your church who are motivated by other models?
5  See if you can propose a rough model of how you would like your

local church to function. Though you may not agree with the Discipleship model as set out in this book, as you react with it, pray that you will clarify your own task as a Christian.

## Prayer
*"Jesus Christ, Lord of the worldwide church, help me to see your plan. Give me a vision of what I have to do, and renew my faith to do it."*

## Footnotes

[1] James Watson, *The Double Helix: A Personal Account of the Structure of DNA*, (New York: Atheneum, 1968).

[2] Thomas S. Kuhn, *The Structure of Scientific Revolutions*, 2nd. Edition, (Chicago: University of Chicago Press, 1970), p. 4. Kuhn has been attacked in various ways, and has had to qualify his use of the term "paradigm," but the importance of paradigms and models has profoundly affected the philosophy of science.

[3] In his book, *Models of the Church*, (New York: Doubleday & Co., 1974), Avery Dulles worked with five models of the Church: as Institution, as Mystical Communion, as Sacrament, as Herald, as Servant. Where his models illustrate the nature of the church as a whole, I have concentrated on churches more at the point of their taking in and teaching new members.

[4] Ludwig Wittgenstein, *Philosophical Investigations*, (Oxford: Basil Blackwell), part I, sections 23-27, 31-38, 65-71. The best introduction to the implications of this mode of thinking is Donald Hudson's *Ludwig Wittgenstein: The Bearing of his Philosophy upon Religious Belief*, (London: Lutterworth Press, 1968). Peter Winch was the first to note the importance of Wittgenstein's thinking for the social sciences: *The Idea of a Social Science: and its Relation to Philosophy*, (New York: Humanities Press, 1963).

[5] A form of the probationary model had been adopted in some church circles by the end of the second century, as, for example, that of Hippolytus (c. AD 170-236), see *Apostolic Tradition*, Gregory Dix ed., (London: SPCK, 1937). I will be arguing that there is no trace of a period of probation to be seen in the New Testament baptisms. Many modern discussions of Christian initiation are flawed by the careless assumption that Hippolytus' model of baptism is a continuation of what the early churches practiced. It is in fact a serious perversion.

[6] Although huge numbers of Christians in the Roman Catholic, Greek Orthodox, and Anglican churches have for long periods of time maintained variants of these models, modern theologians in all these churches would prefer to avoid an *ex opere operato* view of the sacrament. As we will see, the Discipleship model enables us to give force to the instrumental nature of the baptismal texts without the magical connotation which we find so difficult.

[7] Kuhn, *op cit.*, pp. 10-11, 24, 47.

[8] Kuhn, *op. cit.*, pp. 17-18, 81.

[9] The progress of the debate in the last forty years is outlined in the chronological bibliography at the back of this book. A cursory glance at this will indicate the incredible lack of unanimity among scholars. I have failed to find a good presentation of baptism from the eschatalogical point of view, which, with its variants, further complicates the modern theological scene. This is taught in Canada, for example, by Dr. Oliver O'Donovan at Wycliffe College of the University of Toronto.

# Disciples

*Go therefore and make
disciples of all nations . . .
teaching them to observe all
that I have commanded you
(Matt. 28:19, 20).*

## 2

FOR OVER THIRTY YEARS I HAVE BEEN COMPELLED by a passion to obey the Great Commission of Jesus Christ. The words "go," "make disciples," "teach" have again and again governed my best motives, though with many failures of vision in between. The Great Commission took me first into theological training, then overseas for eleven years as a field missionary. Finally it forced me into writing and rewriting this book in the context of the busy pastoral work of three Canadian parishes. Gradually the work of making disciples, and teaching them, has crystallized into a model, which gives me a clear picture of who is to be baptized, and why, and what should follow. This way of picturing my task seems to make sense of the many, often confusing, references to baptism in the New Testament, and to my mind it solves many difficulties in the current discussions of baptism, church membership, discipline, and church growth.

In this Discipleship model, the key concept is that of "making disciples" which is the meaning of the Greek verb *matheteusate* used in the Great Commission. Jesus Christ taught his own disciples for three years. Before leaving them he told the apostles to go and make other disciples among the nations. The main work of the Church is, therefore, to make disciples, and then to teach them all that Jesus would want them to learn. That may seem very obvious, even simplistic, but it has profound implications which have generally been ignored.

## What Is a Disciple?

The word "disciple" means a learner, someone who is learning to do something, or to be something, with the help of a teacher. In this sense, Christians are people who are learning with the help of Jesus Christ, or, we may say, learning from the Holy Spirit.

Another way of looking at learning is to think of God as our Father, and ourselves as his children. Why should Jesus tell us to pray to "our Father" and to be like children in his family? One reason is that every loving father wants and helps his children to learn. He encourages crawling, talking, walking, the three Rs, music, art, sports, and other skills, and the general attitudes towards people and things that the child may need for a full and happy life. This task in a human family is facilitated because normal children are incredibly teachable. They have the genetic equipment to begin learning from their earliest days. They exercise their muscles, look at anything new, touch whatever moves or attracts their attention. They love stories and play, and they are wonderful mimics. In an area where several languages are spoken they can master all of them with ease, using the dialect, tone, and facial expressions appropriate for each.

## The Christian Church: a Loving Family

Thus, whether we think of being disciples or of being children of God, the ideas of learning and of being teachable are prominent. Childlike curiosity and eagerness to learn are the qualities most needed for Christian discipleship. Or, to put it another way, churches are meant to be places where ordinary people can have their curiosity about God, and their eagerness to learn the things of the Spirit, easily satisfied. It should be as easy to learn from Jesus Christ in a church as it is for children in a loving family to learn. That was how the first disciples began their learning.

In the Gospels we find Jesus preaching and healing the crowds because he had compassion on them. But his main work before the resurrection was to make disciples and to instruct them. His invitation was for people to come, "take my yoke upon you, and learn of me." After being empowered by the Holy Spirit the disciples were, in turn, to make disciples in all nations.

## Discipling and Teaching

It is easy to see that the book of Acts provides us with a picture of the Holy Spirit continuing the work of making and training disciples, a work which Jesus had begun. One of the principles for determining the purpose of an ancient book is to see how the book begins and how it ends. Luke begins his first chapter by stressing the continuance of the teaching work of Jesus. "In the first book, O Theophilus, I have dealt with all that Jesus began to do and teach." The last chapter similarly emphasizes the preaching and teaching of Jesus: "[Paul] lived there two whole years ... preaching the kingdom of God and teaching about the Lord Jesus quite openly and unhindered."

If we trace Luke's use of the words *didaskein, didache, didaskalia* it becomes obvious that the emphasis on teaching, which occurs in the first and last verses of Acts, is of very great interest to the writer. For example:

2:42 "...they devoted themselves to the apostles' teaching...."

4:2 "...annoyed because they were teaching the people...."

4:18 "They...charged them not to speak or teach...."

5:21 "...they entered the temple at daybreak and taught."

5:25 "The men whom you put in prison are...teaching the people."

5:28 "...you have filled Jerusalem with your teaching...."

5:42 "...every day in the temple and at home they did not cease teaching and preaching Jesus as the Christ."

Luke describes how the world-wide spread of Jesus' teaching began after the day of Pentecost, when three thousand new learners were baptized and thus added to the previous disciples whom Jesus had taught. Immediately after their baptism they "devoted themselves to the apostles' teaching" (Luke 2:42).

It was this large-scale teaching activity that so upset the religious authorities. "The priests and the captain of the temple and the Sadducees came upon them, annoyed because they were teaching the people" (Acts 4:1, 2). "They set them before the council. And the high priest questioned them, saying, 'We strictly charged you not to teach in this name, yet here you have filled Jerusalem with your teaching'" (Acts 5:27, 28). In spite of threats, imprisonment, and beatings, the instruction of disciples continued. Throughout the book of Acts we see the work of discipling, which started in Jerusalem, continuing exactly according to Jesus' command given at the end of Matthew's gospel.

In Antioch, for example, there were so many people wanting to be taught that Barnabas went to look for Saul, who was then living in Tarsus, to come and help in the work of instruction. Then we read that "for a whole year they met with the church, and taught a large company of people; and in Antioch the disciples were, for the first time, called Christians" (Acts 11:25-27). If we translate this as "in Antioch the learners were for the first time called Christians" we will realize that the first definition of the word "Christian" is *someone who is learning about Jesus Christ.* Too often we have given the word a quite different meaning. We have managed to suggest that a Christian is someone who has attained certain standards of goodness, or had special mystical experiences, or made some great decisions, or understands a particular set of doctrines. But we must emphasize that a Christian church is first of all a group of learners. Christians are not saints who have arrived, but children who are learning.

## Other Images of the Church

The hundreds of references to disciples, learning, teaching, doctrine, and instruction, reinforce the concept of Christian churches as schools. This view obviously permeates the New Testament.[1] Other images of the Church are sometimes presented, metaphors such as a temple of living stones, the body and the bride of Christ, a household, a family, a city, a kingdom, a fellowship, a called-out people. The school model is admittedly not named as such, but its importance seems to outweigh all the others, for it was in this underlying framework of teaching and learning that the Christians viewed their task.[2]

## What Makes a School?

That churches are schools may seem obvious enough, but the idea of comparing a church to a school may evoke very negative reactions. Words like "teaching" and "learning" may suggest hard work, long hours, and boring classes. A school may be thought of as a place where a stern teacher with a rod drums Latin verbs into little boys, or where a

medieval professor lectures on propositions from Euclid
and Aristotle to his pupils. In fact, Christian teaching is
very different. It is no mere cerebral imparting of intellectual knowledge under conditions of rigorous discipline,
but is much more akin to the continuous, almost unrecog-
nized education that goes on in a loving family. A child
does not learn by memorizing propositions about life. He
eats with his parents, plays with them and with his
brothers and sisters, gets kissed and cuddled, copies the
behavior and manners of the home, shares in decision
making, moral judgments, happy times and disasters,
chores and kindnesses. Discipline may be involved, but
only as one of a number of continuous, shared experiences
in the family.

When I began my ministry after three years of theological studies, I pictured my work simply as the imparting of
Christian doctrines. It seemed clear that each person
needed to be taught about God and man, sin and salvation,
faith and repentance, and at every point objections had to
be answered, and erroneous tendencies had to be exposed
and corrected. Such teaching was very much a theological
and cerebral activity. I dread to think of the impression
I must have given, and how far I was from the spirit and
reality of what the Gospels suggest.

## Jesus' Teaching Methods

I am not sure when it first dawned on me that Jesus never
taught doctrines except by way of answers to questions.
And now, instead of propositional truth, I try to teach
beginners how to talk to God, how to tell him their doubts
and problems, how to thank him. I want to teach them how
to forgive and accept forgiveness, how to love their
enemies, and how to love their wives or husbands, children or parents. I try to be practical about how each should
serve, submit to others, develop personal gifts or talents,

cope with strong emotions, use money, and find the way around the Bible for a balanced diet. Doctrine, in the sense of abstract theological statement, comes later.[3]

I was impressed by the portrayal of Jesus in the musical *Godspell* where he teaches his disciples like children. There was so much singing, and fun, and laughter, and being loved. I like it when people pray as simply as little children talking to their parents. Of course, children have quarrels, and for a moment they may not be on speaking terms, but five minutes later they make up and go on as if nothing had happened. I want Christians to learn to forgive one another as quickly as that. Much of our childhood learning time is spent in developing language skills, and I view the Bible as designed to teach little children the ways of God in the language of God. The Old and New Testaments are a library with all that we need for every stage of our discipleship.

At the center of our family life is the dining room with its bread and wine. The children and members of a family have a right to come to the family table. Others need to be invited. In a way it is the pattern of regularly eating together that constitutes a loving family, and as a child grows, much of the learning, developing of attitudes, and discussion of moral values takes place at table, at a family meal. That is why Jesus did so much of his teaching at table, and he told his disciples to keep meeting at their communion table. He told them that he would be there, and there the Holy Spirit would lead them into truth. So, around the bread and wine we share in family thanksgiving, singing, rich symbols and dramatic acts, the kiss of peace, family love, prayer for our needs and the things that concern us. The idea that education at its best occurs around a common table has often been suggested.[4] The Church, in obedience to her Lord, has continued this kind of education for twenty centuries.

## Children in Church

A major turning point in my thinking was the realization
that in a family children eat and drink, are loved and
played with, sing songs, and recite jingles, long before
they know cerebrally what these activities signify. Such
an insight has tremendous implications for the presence
of children at our communion services.[5] We share at the
family table, and subconsciously learn from being accepted there, before we understand what a family is. The
idea of responsibility and commitment to our family and
its ideals comes much later.

Gradually I have come to see that Christ's way of teaching and learning—education in a family atmosphere—is
far, far removed from academic theology.[6] And of course
our schools for disciples have nothing to do with hard
benches, rote learning, wearisome classes, and the
trauma of examinations. Although I would like the church
to have the atmosphere of a happy kindergarten, I would
still insist that, according to the Great Commission for the
Church, our gatherings must grow into schools where
disciples are to learn all that Jesus taught.

### Questions for Study and Discussion

1  In the Preface, the author told the story of his entrance into Christian discipleship. Jot down the main steps in the process of your
   own learning from God.
2  In Antioch the disciples were for the first time called "Christians"
   (Acts 11:25-27). The author comments "A Christian church is first
   a group of learners." What is the usual definition of the word
   "Christian" among those who don't go to church? What is your
   definition?
3  The idea of comparing a church to a school may evoke a very negative reaction. Why do some children hate school? Are there similar
   reasons for hating churches?
4  Can learning ever be a happy experience? Could your church
   become a happy place to learn about God? What kinds of changes
   would be needed?
5  Children learn by doing things in a family long before their minds

can understand what these activities mean. What are the implications for this in the elements of Christian worship: hymns, psalms, prayers, holy communion?

## Prayer

*"O God, my Father, help me to be excited about learning like a little child. I would love our church to be a happy place. Bless our Christian family as a home for disciples."*

## Footnotes

1 After a study of various ancient schools such as the schools of Pythagorus, the Academy, the Lyceum, the Garden of Epicurus, the Stoa, Qumran, the schools of the disciples of Hillel and Philo, the conclusion that Jesus and his disciples formed a school is found in R. Alan Culpepper's *The Johannine School: An Evaluation of the Johannine School Hypothesis Based on an Investigation of the Nature of Ancient Schools,* (Missoula, Montana: Scholars Press, 1975 [1974 Duke University Ph.D. thesis]), p. 215.

2 See for example: Ian A. Muirhead, *Education in the New Testament,* edited by C. Ellis Nelson, (New York: Association Press, 1965).

3 Some implications of this kind of training are set out by Morton Kelsey in *Can Christians Be Educated? A .Proposal for Effective Communication of our Christian Religion,* (Mishawaka, Indiana: Religious Education Press Inc., 1977).

4 For hundreds of years the first requirement for graduation at Oxford and Cambridge Universities has been the eating of so many meals in a college hall. It was at King Arthur's round table that his knights were educated.

5 See Urban T. Holmes, *Young Children and the Eucharist,* (New York: Seabury Press, 1972).

6 Ian Stuchbery's excellent discussion entitled "How We Grow in Christ—Ideas from the Fields of Psychology and Education", is found in *Growing in Christ: New Patterns of Initiation and Education in the Parish Community,* (Toronto: Anglican Book Centre, 1978), pp. 43-50.

# Baptism

*Go therefore and make
disciples of all nations,
baptizing them in the name
of the Father and of the
Son and of the Holy Spirit
(Matt. 28:19).*

## 3

AS WE CONTINUE TO DISCUSS THE GREAT COMMISSION of Jesus Christ, we must now focus on the words "make" and "baptizing." *Disciples had to be made* before they could be taught. That means that Christian teaching was not to be a part of the general education of the whole of society. Learners needed to be formally enrolled. If you want your kids to start kindergarten you must take them to the school and register them. You can't study at any evening school, or art college, or local high school without being enrolled. The enrollment may be very simple, such as attending the first class and giving your name and address. For advanced work you may need to present transcripts of previous work done, and for enrollment in a graduate school, only select and qualified students will be accepted. But in our society we are all familiar with the idea that it is only the registered learners who will be taught. There may be a few unregistered auditors but they are the exceptions. Teachers *teach* only students on their authorized list.

This is also a familiar principle in the East. In India, for example, a teacher of religious subjects is called a *guru*. He accepts as disciples those who come and learn with him. He does not teach just anyone, but only those who are his own enrolled learners. Other people in the community may come to him for advice, they may ask questions, and they might even sit in on some of his classes or public lectures, but they are not his disciples.

Similarly, in the Gospels we find that the personal disciples of Jesus were very clearly marked off from other groups of disciples. For example, "John's disciples and the Pharisees were fasting, and people came and said to him, 'Why do John's disciples and the disciples of the Pharisees fast, but your disciples do not fast?' " (Mark 2:18). Here we have three distinct groupings, the disciples of John the Baptist, the disciples of Jesus, and the disciples of the Pharisees. Though it is not specifically stated, it seems probable that each rabbi among the Pharisees had his own recognized group of learners. There were thus schools of disciples, and people knew who and how many had joined each group. "When the Lord knew that the Pharisees had heard that Jesus was making and baptizing more disciples than John (although Jesus himself did not baptize, but only his disciples), he left Judea" (John 4:1-3).

## Who Were Jesus' Disciples?

This large increase in the number of Jesus' disciples also indicates that it was not only the twelve apostles who were disciples of Jesus during his three years of ministry.[1] In some cases disciples were fickle and lost interest. Thus, after Jesus' teaching about eating his flesh and drinking his blood (which was admittedly shocking to Jewish ears) "many of his disciples drew back and no longer went about with him" (John 6:66). There were also secret disciples. Joseph of Arimathea is mentioned in all four Gospels as the man who took Jesus down from the cross and buried him. In Matthew's gospel he is called "a disciple of Jesus" and John's gospel adds "but secretly for fear of the Jews." In any case, whether secretly or openly, as loyal, long-term learners or as fickle turncoats, there seems to have been a definite enrollment of disciples among the learners of Jesus, and it was these who received the deeper instruction which was not given to the crowds. Parables were for the crowd, but only to the enrolled learners did Jesus give explanations. "With many such parables he spoke the word to them, as they were able to hear it; he did not speak to them without a parable, but privately to his own disciples he explained everything" (Mark 4:33-34).

### The Plan and Practice of Baptism
Now, according to our text, Jesus expected his apostles to continue the practice of enrolling disciples. Disciples were made by baptism, and it was the baptized who were to be taught. "Go therefore and make disciples of all nations, baptizing them . . . and teaching them to observe all that I have commanded you." As we will see, Jesus' method was continued in the early church in Jerusalem and in the churches planted by Paul. After the crowds had been preached to, those who wished to learn were quickly baptized, and then the intensive teaching began in churches which functioned as schools for the baptized.[2] At first this sounds simple. In all Christian denominations, except the Salvation Army and most Quakers, some form of baptism is used to enroll people. And in all churches, most of the teaching is given to those who are already baptized. Why then do different denominations differ so bitterly as to mode, and time, and candidates for baptism?

## The Modes and Their Meaning

The reason for misunderstanding is that baptism is a sign
which has many meanings. Take, as an analogy, the
raising of my right hand. The meaning of such an action is
determined largely by its context. In the middle of the
road it means "Stop!" In a classroom it probably indicates
that I have a question. Passing by a friend on the opposite
side of the street, I am saying "Hi!" In a committee
meeting I indicate that I am in favor of a motion. And at
an auction, after the question "Will anyone offer me $25?"
my raised hand will buy me the white elephant, unless
someone else makes a better bid. If we were living in a
small town with no school, or traffic, or auctions, or committee meetings, we would recognize that raising one's
right hand means "Hi" but we wouldn't know of its other
meanings. That is why Christians who are raised in one
narrow, sheltered church circle find different modes of
baptism in other churches so disconcerting.

## Baptism—a Worldwide Religious Phenomenon

The use of water as a sign has dozens of functions among
various world religions. Along the banks of the river
Ganges in India, millions of people take a baptism every
day. Each sect of Hinduism, and every *guru,* will attach a
slightly different interpretation to baptism in the Ganges.
At the time of Jesus the Jewish people were familiar with
all sorts of baptisms among the heathen people around
them. In Crete there used to be a baptism in the blood of a
bull. The mystery religions of Greece used washing for
various forms of initiation. Among the Jews the sect of the
Essenes practiced baptisms. The monks of the Qumran
monastery who may have reared John the Baptist,
collected and hid what are now known as the Dead Sea
Scrolls. These scrolls refer to baptisms, and the monastery
itself had a baptistry.

The variety of meanings of baptism has multiplied since

the establishment of the early church. Some view baptism as a means of removing original sin from babies. Many people think of a christening as the proper occasion to gather one's friends to celebrate with a party. Other groups, including Baptists, make it an occasion of public witness to a new-found faith. Often churches have used baptism as a reward for perseverance during many months of instruction and good behavior. In nations where Christians are a persecuted minority, the rite is viewed as a proof of apostasy, a rejection of a traditional religion in order to join a new brotherhood.

According to our text, Jesus intended the sign of baptism to signify the enrolling of learners. Though most churches would concur, the agreement quickly turns to disagreement when we ask the question: Who should be baptized? If we use the school analogy again, do we enroll all candidates, or only those who first prove themselves, or who attain a certain age, or who understand and believe certain things, or those who have proved their commitment by good behavior and perseverance?

This problem arises wherever there are teachers and disciples of any kind. In Japan, a famous Judo instructor might accept only those who already have a black belt, or those with some particular moral or physical qualities. Or he might accept only young boys who have had no previous instruction. He might also require a probationary period to ensure the commitment of his pupils before they became official disciples, or he might make becoming a disciple easy and only later expel those who did not measure up.

What is striking about the early churches described in the book of Acts is that they seemed to take in anybody! Since all baptisms were immediate,[3] there was obviously no time to investigate the new disciples, no probationary period to weed out the good from the bad. Disciples were baptized first and *then* taught. This was certainly the case

with Jesus' first twelve disciples. They knew little of
Christian behavior or doctrine when they began. I will
argue in a later chapter that the twelve disciples were
baptized by Jesus at the beginning of his ministry since
there is no other record of their baptism. At least one of
the first twelve turned out to be a rogue, and even the best
of them failed pretty miserably.

According to the parable of the sower there is no way
at the time when God's truth is first received, that we can
ascertain whether an individual's faith is going to be
genuine. Some will quit learning the next day, others will
begin with great enthusiasm and then lose interest. The
thorns of care and worry will choke the growth of many,
and only a small proportion will produce the acceptable
fruits of discipleship. In view of this there were two
courses open to Peter and the other apostles on the day of
Pentecost. They could either watch candidates for baptism
for a long time until there was reasonable certainty that
they were going to be good wheat. (And how long would
most of us have to be watched?) Or they could take in all
comers, teach them, and expect to harvest a proportion of
good wheat in due course.[4]

## Adding to the Churches

A characteristic expression for baptizing disciples in the
book of Acts is "adding." "Those who received his word
were baptized, and there were added that day about three
thousand souls . . . and the Lord added to their number
day by day those who were being saved" (Acts 2:41, 47).
As a minister of the church of Jesus Christ I am interested
in "adding," but I may have questions about what should
be required before baptism. Who are to be added? How
should they be selected? Are there qualifications, or pre-
requisites, or proper attitudes of mind necessary before
baptism? The next reference to "adding" might be cited to
prove that only believers should be baptized. "And more

than ever, believers were added to the Lord, multitudes both of men and women" (Acts 5:14). But then I ask myself whether believers are any different from learners, and if so, what should they have believed, and how should their faith be tested?

We have noted that, although churches were to be beautiful centers of the activity of the Holy Spirit, there was apparently no attempt made to exclude unsuitable candidates. What are the implications of this extraordinary receptiveness? A society which admitted all comers without question surely would destroy itself. And can we conceive of quality education taking place in a school where any pupils were accepted regardless of age or experience in learning, and without any consideration of their suitability or commitment?

### The Upheaval at Philippi

Consider, for example, the Philippian jailer. He was a civil servant charged with the custody of Paul and Silas, so "he put them into the inner prison and fastened their feet in stocks." He may have heard his two prisoners singing hymns. At midnight he awoke to find that an earthquake had so shaken the prison that all the doors had swung open and the fetters had broken off. Imagining that a mass escape had taken place, the jailor was about to commit suicide, when one of his prisoners, Paul, told him not to harm himself—all the inmates were still safely inside. Obviously shaken, he brought Paul and Silas out of the prison and asked them what he had to do to be saved. They assured him that by believing in the Lord Jesus he would be saved, together with his household. After brief instruction "he was baptized at once with all his family" (Acts 16:25-35).

Now, even if we suppose that the Philippian jailer had previously heard Paul's preaching, would it not have been wise to see if this emotional, earthquake repentance was

likely to be permanent? And what of his household? Even
if we assume that they were all adult family members and
slaves, and all had had a chance to hear what being baptized meant, and all accepted baptism and Christian
discipleship of their own free will, the suddenness of their
enrollment is still surprising; the whole household is baptized between midnight and breakfast! There was certainly no time to investigate their character. Nor did it
seem necessary to check out their good intentions, or
obtain assurance that they would all persevere in their
teaching. Evidently it was the jailor's decision that was
decisive. He wanted them all to learn about the Jesus that
Paul preached, and that was sufficient. Similarly, when
Lydia, the businesswoman from Philippi, opened her
heart to Paul's preaching, she was quickly baptized, with
her household. For the three thousand on the day of Pentecost there was no probation, no checking out the reality of
the faith of the baptized. Baptism was immediate and
what counted was the instruction given by the Holy Spirit
to the learners after their enrollment.

The fact that acceptance into the church was to be open
to all without question was also clearly implied in the
parables of Jesus. In Matthew's account of the marriage
feast, the first invited guests did not bother to come, so
others were to be invited. "Go therefore to the thorough-
fares and invite to the marriage feast as many as you
find." Jesus expressly adds the words, "And those servants
went out into the streets and gathered all whom they
found, both bad and good" (Matt. 22:9, 10). In Luke's account of the parable the invited guests made trivial
excuses. To take their place, the servant was ordered to
"go out quickly to the streets and lanes of the city, and
bring in the poor and maimed and blind and lame." When
there was still room in the banquet hall, the invitation
was made even more strongly persuasive. "Go out to the
highways and hedges, and compel people to come in, that

my house may be filled" (Luke 14:16-23). In the light of such parables we should not be surprised that the early church took in all comers for instruction and invited them immediately to share in the church's feast.

### Levels of Faith
In answer to this openness we may be tempted to object, "but surely faith must be a prerequisite to baptism." Admittedly the jailer must have believed it was worthwhile for him and his household to learn about Jesus Christ. But how deep could the faith of his family and slaves be at such short notice? In a later chapter we will discuss the theological distinction to be made between the *faith to begin learning* and *justification by faith,* which is the main learning topic in the school after baptism. We will also argue that the New Testament teaches justification by faith, not justification by a decision of faith. Profession of faith is no guarantee of spirituality. "Not every one who says to me, 'Lord, Lord,' shall enter the kingdom of heaven, but he who does the will of my Father" (Matt. 7:21). John's gospel tells us that many of the disciples who decided to follow Jesus when he first began his ministry later "went back" (John 6:66).

From the parable of the sower it seems obvious that a fruitful faith cannot be discerned in the hearer when first the Word of God is heard. In some cases the Word never takes root at all. Others appear to have a joyful faith for a time, but they dry up during trouble or persecution.[5] A third category of disciples have their initial faith choked by the cares and riches of the world, and it is only those disciples who prove to have a genuine faith who hear the Word and understand it, and so prove fruitful (Matt. 13:18-23). If baptisms are to be immediate there is evidently no way to distinguish among these four kinds of disciples. The possibility of some failures is no reason to delay the baptism of all who can be taught.

Another significant parable is that of the net. "Again, the kingdom of heaven is like a net which was thrown into the sea and gathered fish of every kind; when it was full, men drew it ashore and sat down and sorted the good into vessels but threw away the bad. So it will be at the close of the age. The angels will come out and separate the evil from the righteous" (Matt. 13:47-50). It is closely parallel to the parable of the tares in which, again, the sorting out of good and bad is left to God at the close of the age. Meanwhile, we are instructed to refrain from any present attempt to root out the tares, "lest in gathering the weeds you root up the wheat along with them" (Matt. 13:24-29). The early church must have used these parables to explain their enrollment of any seeker in their schools of the Holy Spirit. They accepted the fact that, in adding new disciples, some would eventually turn out bad. But that was not their concern. There was certainly no argument for limiting the catch of fish for fear of taking in some that would eventually be thrown out. As we will see later, the only limitation Scripture makes is the capacity of the net. We have no right to baptize people whom we cannot undertake to teach, but we must not refuse individuals because of their lack of promise.

### Indiscriminate Baptism?
The parables of Jesus therefore seem designed to justify the open admission policy illustrated in the book of Acts. Not only should everyone be included, but in some cases the riffraff of the city might even be compelled to come in to the banquet. That would be sufficient justification for the head of a household to insist that his whole family and all his household slaves be baptized and instructed. As the gospel moved across Europe it was common for a king to be convinced by the missionaries, and then order his whole tribe to be lined up for baptism. Though this may sound like indiscriminate baptism, the picture of the

church as a school for disciples changes the tone of the whole situation. Indiscriminate baptism in its bad sense involves baptizing all and sundry with no provision for "the apostles' teaching and fellowship," worship around the bread and the wine, and "the prayers" (Acts 2:42). Indiscriminate baptism in the right sense requires that any church that baptizes must also provide the rich life of a school of the Holy Spirit for those who are added by baptism. The responsibility to do this lies within the church, not in the good intentions or hesitating faith of the new learners.

**Examination and Teaching**
We have already seen the problems of ascertaining proper faith before baptism, especially if baptisms are to be as immediate as in the New Testament. I have argued that baptism was used to enroll learners. If baptism is into the school of Christ, there is no way we can find out, before they are taught, how learners will respond. They want to learn and that must be sufficient. Any checking up at this point will hinder only the one who comes with a healthy sense of his own limitations. No ordinary examination will prevent the entrance of the self-confident, the badly intentioned, the tares, the false prophets. Once we are committed to taking in any one, however bad, with faith that the Holy Spirit will handle the stubborn and unteachable, then there is no need to introduce unnecessary obstacles to initiation.

In learning to drive we notice the vast difference in mentality between a government driving examiner and a good driving instructor. The examiner has his list of checkpoints, and if the person being tested fails two or three of these he is rejected. I suggest that there is no place for the examiner mentality at the point of baptism. Later I will argue that churches must never pose as examiners of their members in order to throw out those who fail.

The mentality of the driving instructor is quite different. He prides himself on being willing to teach the most hopeless driver. He is not disturbed by previous failures and accidents. Patiently he plans to teach those who cannot drive at all until they learn to drive safely. I have argued that the church is in the business of teaching the worst sinners to live safely, delighting in taking in the most unlikely prospects for heaven, and having no doubt that the Holy Spirit is willing and able to teach them. Later we will see that the early churches, while open to enrolling anyone by baptism, obviously expected higher standards for those who were to function as teachers. Driving schools cannot afford to use as teachers those with poor driving records, or those who encourage their pupils to drag at full speed down the street.

## The Children of Christians

At this point we note two different methods of enrolling the children of parents who have been baptized. Let us assume that the parents come knowing very little of the Christian faith. They want to learn, so we baptize them. They also want their children to learn. One method is to baptize the whole household, whatever the ages of its members. If baptism is to enroll learners, and they are all going to be taught from infancy, then children are as much candidates for the school of Christ as are their parents. This would be the usual method of administering baptism in Anglican, Presbyterian, Orthodox, Roman Catholic, Methodist, Lutheran, and other churches that practice infant baptism. A second method of applying the discipleship model of the church to baptism is to dedicate infants, and then view baptism as the entrance into learning under one's own initiative, say in one's teens. One might compare circumcision as a model for the first method.[6] The *bar mitzvah,* when a boy of thirteen is made a full member of the Jewish community, or the practice of confirmation in some churches, would be comparable to the second method.

We should note first of all that the practice of baptizing the children of Christian parents on the model of confirmation or a *bar mitzvah* is not acceptable to those who take believers' baptism seriously. For them, baptism has nothing to do with becoming a learner, but is rather a witness to one's having accepted Jesus Christ as personal Savior and having thereby experienced the new birth. We will pursue the questions of decisional faith and the new birth in later chapters. Meanwhile, we should recognize some important factors that are common to both our first and second methods of baptizing the children of Christian parents under the Discipleship model.

Regardless of how baptism is administered, most denominations agree that some religious rite is needed soon after birth to express the welcome of the newborn baby into the family of God, either by infant dedication or infant baptism. In either case, the dedication or the baptism of infants is not an end but a beginning of a process of learning under the Holy Spirit. Whether a child is baptized or dedicated from infancy there should be constant learning of the Christian faith by actions, words, songs, Scripture, and worship. Even if there is a clear decision of faith and signs of deep spiritual life are observed, before baptism or confirmation in his teens, a child still has a lifetime of learning by the Holy Spirit ahead of him.

Although I practice the baptism of infants as an Anglican minister, I cannot prove that infants were baptized, say, in the household of Lydia or in the household of the Philippian jailer (Acts 16). Nor does it seem likely that all the children of those baptized on the day of Pentecost were baptized at the same time. Those who delay the baptism of children till they have made a profession of faith cannot prove that the children of Christians in the New Testa-

ment period were dedicated as infants. Nor is there any
way of knowing what happened to the children of Christian parents when they came of age, or puberty, or made
some personal decision to continue in their parents' faith.
All that I have attempted to show is that baptism was
used to enroll adult learners without probation and without delay. Justification by faith and an explanation of how
exactly the crucifixion and resurrection of Christ saved
them was taught to those already baptized, as in the
epistles of Paul. Having settled the basic meaning of baptism as a method of adding disciples to be taught by the
Holy Spirit, we must then decide on the most appropriate
way of administering it in the case of the children of the
baptized. And since we cannot prove conclusively that our
method is the right one, we had better be charitable and
at least listen to each other.

I will be suggesting, from various points of view, that
children should be allowed to share in our communion
services. We no longer maintain the Victorian idea that
children must have learned their manners before they
can eat with their parents. Translated into the context of
the church family, that would mean that either we must
baptize children and view baptism as the normal means of
enrollment, with full rights to communion and worship,
or we should view dedication as giving children the same
right. Adult or believers' baptism, confirmation, admission into full membership, or any other rite can later be
used to indicate entry into adult responsibilities.

**The Source of Power**
It is important that we picture the tremendous faith which
the early Christians had in the transforming power of the
Holy Spirit. What the Holy Spirit was going to do was very
much a part of what was seen in baptism. They could
afford to be totally welcoming at the point of admission
because they had no confidence in the candidates them-

selves. Apart from the work of the Holy Spirit every person, whether Jew or Greek, was viewed as dead (Eph. 2:1 ff.). It was taken for granted that he was unable, of himself, to produce anything of what the school proposed for him. Harriet Auber captured this thought exactly in her hymn:

> *And every virtue we possess,*
> *And every victory won,*
> *And every thought of holiness,*
> *Are his alone.*

If, then, baptism was the introduction into the sphere or school of the Holy Spirit, obviously good or bad qualities, noble or despicable intentions, sincerity or perversity— all were irrelevant before baptism. The whole emphasis was on what *God* was going to do. The Holy Spirit, who was totally responsible for teaching and illuminating the pupils, could be relied on to handle the most unteachable, intractable, degraded human material. The school of Christ was viewed as capable of perfecting the very worst of sinners. The suggestion that some who came, or were brought for baptism, were too fickle, sinful, unmotivated, ignorant, or depraved would have been unthinkable. It would have been an insult to Christ to suggest that anyone was too sinful for him to save.

### Questions for Study and Discussion

1 In our society we are familiar with the idea that only registered learners will be taught. List at least ten secular organizations in your area which register people to learn various skills.

2 Jesus intended baptism to be used to enroll learners. For what other purposes is baptism used in various Christian denominations? (See, for example, the models in the Introduction.)

3 According to the Discipleship model in this book, the parable of the sower describes what happens to disciples after baptism and teaching by the Holy Spirit. What would be needed to make sure we only baptized "good grain"?

4   Baptism was immediate and what counted was the instruction given by the Holy Spirit to the learners after their enrollment. What secular organizations in your community examine candidates before enrollment, and which permit immediate enrollment? What about your own church?

5   Good or bad qualities, noble or despicable intentions, sincerity or perversity, all were irrelevant before baptism. What are the implications of taking in sinners, regardless of their goodness or badness, into Christian churches?

## Prayer
*"O God the Holy Spirit, thank you for what you have done in my life, and in the lives of so many Christians. Help us to bring others into your circle of disciples."*

## Footnotes

[1] Luke's gospel tells us expressly that the twelve apostles were chosen from among a much larger number of disciples (Luke 6:13). He further distinguishes "a great crowd of his disciples" from "a great multitude of people" from all the surrounding areas (Luke 6:17).

[2] In Galatia, on the first missionary journey, the book of Acts distinguishes what Paul did when he "made many disciples" and the later work of "strengthening the souls of the disciples" (Acts 14:21, 22).

[3] It could be argued that there were delays in some cases, but we have no evidence of this, and the epistles of Paul, and the pastoral and other epistles give no instructions about delay or checking the sincerity of candidates. The fact that John records many baptisms of those becoming disciples, and then describes much apostasy, suggests that no screening of candidates took place in the church circles that he was familiar with (John 4:1, 6:60, 66).

[4] Our difficulty is that, although baptisms and baptizing are mentioned, we do not know what other ideas went with the use of water in these cases. There are preachers, candidates, people who perform baptisms, expectations as to who will come for baptism, how they will be accepted or rejected, the mode of baptism, what baptism effects and does not effect, the difference in status before and after, the implied changes of behavior, etc. We cannot take "birth" in those churches and learn the proper context of the form of life in which the words were used. Lexicons do not help at this point. The method used in this book is therefore to construct various models, including one that seems the most elegant, and try these out on the host of specific and indirect references to baptizing and making disciples. Whichever model is adopted, or is being tested, will affect the exegesis of every text that connects with the model. A corollary of this method is that in order to discount it, it is not sufficient to raise difficulties in the model which I propose. If the Discipleship model of baptism solves more problems than any other, it should be adopted unless someone can produce a model that fits the New Testament evidence in a more elegant way. As already indicated, scholars are at hopeless odds at present and this suggests that no existing model of baptism thoroughly fits the evidence.

[5] It seems evident that in the Epistle to the Hebrews apostasy is found among the baptized, who have been "enlightened, who have tasted the heavenly gift, and have become partakers of the Holy Spirit, and have tasted the goodness of the word of God and the powers of the age to come" (Heb. 6:4-6).

[6] The baptism of infants on the analogy of circumcision was argued by Oscar Cullmann, *Baptism in the New Testament*, (London: SCM Press, 1950 [originally in German, 1948]). Pierre Ch. Marcel expressed the point in this way: "To overthrow completely notions so vital, impressed for more than two thousand years on the soul of the people, to withdraw from children the sacrament of admission to the covenant, the Apostolic Church ought to have received from the Lord *an explicit prohibition*, so revolutionary in itself that a record of it would have been preserved in the New Testament" (Philip Edgcumbe Hughes, trans., *The Biblical Doctrine of Infant Baptism*, London: James Clarke & Co., 1953), p. 191, (originally written in French, *Le Baptême*, 1950). John Murray says: "If infants are excluded now, it cannot be too strongly emphasized that this change implies a complete reversal of the earlier divinely instituted practice" (*Christian Baptism*, Philadelphia: Orthodox Presbyterian Church, 1952), p. 52.

# Repentance

*John the Baptist said to the
multitudes that came out to be
baptized" . . . bear fruits that
befit repentance" (Luke 3:7).
Peter said to them, "Repent and
be baptized every one of you in the
name of Jesus Christ"
(Acts 2:38).*

# 4

THE DECISION TO USE THE OPEN admission policy apparently typical of the churches of the New Testament raises
a serious objection which must be faced: "Surely repentance and faith were and are required." I propose to look at
the place of repentance in our ministry in this chapter,
and then discuss the various meanings of the word "faith"
in the next.

The texts at the head of this chapter indicate that John
the Baptist preached a message of repentance, which was
continued in the preaching of Jesus (Mark 1:15). Repentance was also required by Peter of his listeners on the day
of Pentecost. How may I reconcile the open admission
policy of the discipleship model of baptism with this
emphasis on repentance? To answer this we must distinguish some different meanings of the word "repent."

## Three Meanings of "Repentance"

Consider, first of all, the idea of repentance in sackcloth and ashes. Job said, "I despise myself, and repent in dust and ashes" (Job 42:6). Here it looks as if the ashes were a visible expression of deep self-loathing. Jesus said that if the cities of Tyre and Sidon had seen his mighty works "they would have repented long ago, sitting in sackcloth and ashes" (Luke 10:13). In the Church, this kind of repentance is usually called *penitence or contrition.* I am going to argue that this has nothing to do with the kind of repentance which is connected with baptism. Seasons of deep conviction of sin, contrition, and penitence will be inevitable as our Christian experience deepens following baptism. In my own experience, my first turning to learn among God's people was early in October 1947, after leaving the army to study at Cambridge University. It was not until Easter of the following year when I attended a student conference that I began to see the extent of what was wrong in me and what Jesus Christ did on the cross to deal with it. This, I suspect, is the experience of most Christians. The sense of contrition is a comparatively late fruit which seldom appears in the first few hours of instruction. How then could it be made a requirement, when large numbers were suddenly added to the Church for teaching?

The second meaning of repentance is that of *changing one's mind,* and/or regretting one's past attitudes or actions. Thus the King James Version states that "it repented the Lord that he had made man," which is properly changed to "the Lord was sorry" in the RSV (Gen. 6:7). Though theologians may find it difficult to explain how God could be said to change his mind, or regret an action, it should be obvious enough that God is not repenting in sackcloth and ashes in such references.[1] When God was concerned in case the children of Israel might "repent when they see war, and return to Egypt" (Exod. 13:17),

the Hebrew verb *nakham* is the same as in the case of
Job's contrition, but the sense is totally different.[2] Similarly in the Gospel we read of the son who first refused to
work for his father, and then "repented and went" (Matt.
21:29). There is no need to introduce the thought of breast-
beating, self-flagellation, or tearful contrition: the boy
merely changed his mind, and began to work. In the case
of Judas' repentance (Matt. 27:3) there may have been
either a note of penitence, or merely of regret or change
of mind. He certainly did not turn to learn from God,
which is the sense of the term when connected with baptism.

Third, we have the idea of *turning in a different direction,* or to something different, or towards someone. The
Hebrew verb *shub* (return, turn, turn back) is translated
"repented" in Solomon's great prayer at the dedication of
the temple. "If they lay it to heart in the land to which they
have been carried captive, and repent; . . . if they repent
with all their mind," then God will hear and forgive
(1 Kings 8:47-49). This Hebrew verb has no connotations
of sackcloth-and-ashes penitence, nor of change of mind,
but of decisively turning in the direction of God. I suggest
that the repentance spoken of by John the Baptist and
the repentance connected with Christian baptism is a
turning toward God, and in particular a turning *to learn*
from him.

The second sense of repentance, meaning a change of
mind, or regret, is expressed in the New Testament by
the Greek verb *metamelomai.*[3] The verb *metanoeo* and the
noun *metanoia* can mean *either* the sackcloth-and-ashes
type of penitence, or simply a turning or change of direction to learn from God. Which of these two meanings is
connected with baptism must be determined by what
actually took place. In particular we must ask what signs
of repentance were looked for. Did the apostles, and John
the Baptist before them, look for evidence of deep heart

penitence and contrition before baptism, or did they baptize those who were simply turning to learn from God? It
is by discovering what kind of behavior preceded baptism
that the question must be settled.

## John the Baptist's Requirements

It has generally been assumed that John the Baptist
looked for evidence of contrition, or fruits of repentance,
before he baptized those who came to him. But how would
he carry out such an investigation? "And there went out
to him all the country of Judea, and all the people of
Jerusalem; and they were baptized by him in the river
Jordan" (Mark 1:5). There is no need to make "all" mean
every single man, women, and child in Judea and Jerusalem, but at least it means a considerable number of
people. How does one look for fruits of repentance in such
a vast crowd?

Many also take it for granted that John the Baptist turned
away the Pharisees and Sadducees who were coming to
him for baptism. " . . . when he saw many of the Pharisees
and Saducees coming for baptism, he said to them, "You
brood of vipers! Who warned you to flee from the wrath to
come? Bear fruit that befits repentance, and do not pre-
sume to say to yourselves, 'We have Abraham as our
father;' for I tell you, God is able from these stones to raise
up children to Abraham. Even now the axe is laid to the
root of the trees; every tree therefore that does not bear
good fruit is cut down and thrown into the fire" (Matt.
3:7-10; Luke 3:7-9). Thus David Pawson writes, without
justifying his assertion, that "John the Baptist delayed
baptism by sending the candidates away until their lives
showed more evidence of being ready."[4] Quite apart from
the huge problem of doing such an investigation, the sense
of the passage is quite different. A literal translation
would be: "The crowds kept coming out to be baptized, and
he told them to produce fruits worthy of their change of

direction" (Luke 3:7-8). The natural consequence was that as a result of John's preaching people all over the country realized that they were in no fit state to welcome the Messiah. They came to John wanting to learn how to prepare, and he baptized them, enrolling them in his school so that they could learn to turn their lives toward their coming Messiah. They would then remain for several days by the river Jordan as John explained to them the kind of behavior which was appropriate.[5]

In Luke's account of John the Baptist's teaching we are given examples of what people in general were to do, as well as what people in specific professions such as tax collectors and soldiers were to do. In each case the appropriate behavior would have to be put into practice back in their homes and in their jobs: sharing with the needy, avoiding extortion in tax collecting, avoiding violence. Surely John did not send spies back with them to see if they actually did this before letting them present themselves for baptism! Thus baptism was immediate and was followed by teaching as to what was required of the baptized, and the people would then go home to practice what they had been taught. Matthew tells us that John spoke strong words to the Pharisees and Sadducees who came to him for baptism, but there is no suggestion that he refused to baptize them and sent them home to improve first. The repentance connected with John's baptism is a turning to be taught, not a penitence to be evidenced by sufficient contrition. How on earth would one check up on "sufficient contrition"?

### Repentance in Paul's Ministry

We can now see that repentance has the same meaning in the practice of baptism all the way from John the Baptist to the apostolic baptism in the book of Acts. We begin with Paul's account of his preaching to King Agrippa: "that they should repent and turn to God and perform deeds

worthy of their repentance."[6] Were these deeds appropriate to repentance investigated as evidence that the
hearers were now fit for baptism? Evidently not, as we
concluded in previous chapters, since all the recorded
baptisms were immediate.

The worthy deeds and appropriate behavior were
taught to the disciples or learners *after* baptism. They
were the necessary outcome and consequence of learning
from Christ by the Holy Spirit. Thus Paul claims to have
persuaded people to turn away from the teaching of the
idol temples, false religions, Judaizing religion, or other
forms of heterodoxy, to turn to learn from God. Examples
of such turning are found at Lystra in Acts 14:15, and in
the founding of the church in Thessalonica: "you turned
to God from idols" (1 Thess. 1:9). And once the turning had
taken place, and the hearers had been persuaded to enroll
in the church by baptism, they were taught the appropriate conduct for living in this new way.[7]

The idea of turning to learn a new way is very familiar
to modern man. People turn to astrology, and begin
learning about horoscopes. Many have turned from dead
Christian churches to TM or to a Hindu guru for help in
learning to meditate. Why should it only be the oriental
religions, scientology, and other cults which enroll disciples? They charge a fee, which learners are glad to pay. We
put them off with confused ideas about repentance, and
demand that they swallow doctrine and adopt behavior
which most of us learn with difficulty in a lifetime.

### Turning and Baptism

Paul reminded the Ephesian elders that he had testified
to Jews and Greeks "of repentance to God and of faith in
our Lord Jesus Christ" (Acts 20:21). The literal translation is "the into God repentance," or even more simply
"the turning to God." The idea of turning to God as a
verbal equivalent for being baptized, or becoming a Chris-

tian, or becoming a disciple, is found in the book of Acts. James said, "My judgment is that we should not trouble those of the Gentiles who turn to God" (Acts 15:19). We have an example of two whole towns becoming Christians: "And all the residents of Lydda and Sharon saw him, and they turned to the Lord" (Acts 9:35). Similarly the first baptisms and the establishment of the church in Antioch is described by the words "a great number that believed turned to the Lord" (Acts 11:21).

On the Baptist model it is suggested that each one of these large numbers of people made an informed and individual act of faith. But we have already seen that the actual baptisms described in the book of Acts were immediate, without any probation or catechumenate, so there was no time to examine a change of behavior before baptism. What is stressed is that there was tremendous teaching activity *after* the turning. "A large company was added to the Lord. So Barnabas went to Tarsus to look for Saul; and when he had found him, he brought him to Antioch. For a whole year they met with the church, and taught a large company of people; and in Antioch the disciples were for the first time called Christians" (Acts 11:24-26). The natural interpretation is that in these mass or group movements people in considerable numbers turned to learn from Jesus Christ; they were enrolled by baptism; and they were then taught intensively for a long period.[8]

## Motivation for Baptism
This explains why the proclamation of the resurrection was so important as a motive for baptism. Who would turn to learn from a bunch of uneducated Galileans, whose leader had recently been ignominiously crucified? If, however, Jesus was recognized not only as the one who had taught up and down the country for three years, but also as the one who was attested as God's Messiah by the resur-

rection, then the situation was very different. Further-
more Jesus was still alive, in personal control of his new
schools of disciples, and present to teach, through his own
Spirit, wherever they gathered and in whatever language.

The evidence of this was that the ascended Christ had
given the Holy Spirit, not just to a few picked prophets,
as in the Old Testament, but to all the men and women,
boys and girls, who were willing to learn in these amazing
new schools. The apostolic preaching, therefore, first
announced that the risen Messiah was now teaching in
person by the Holy Spirit. Those who believed the proclamation and wished to be taught turned to be enrolled as
disciples by baptism. Immediately there followed the
intensive teaching of all who had thus been added to the
church.

### Can Repentance Be a Subject of Examination?
Another consideration seems to me to be decisive. We
know that Peter and several others of the disciples had
been disciples of John before they followed Jesus. Let us
assume that John did have some system of checking up on
worthy deeds before baptizing the multitudes who came to
him. Let us also assume that Jesus approved this investigation and the rejection of all the unworthy, and that he
continued this practice in the baptisms performed by his
disciples. Then came the day of Pentecost, and three
thousand asked for baptism on one day. If he had been
trained so rigorously by both John and Jesus in ascertaining fruits before baptism, how could Peter suddenly
baptize so many, so suddenly, and without apparently
rejecting anyone? Merely to pose the question in this way
surely reduces our first two assumptions to absurdity.

The natural interpretation of the baptisms on the day of
Pentecost, and the previous ones by John the Baptist and
Jesus' disciples, is that there was no investigation before
baptism. The baptized were taught in the fellowship of

their teacher the fruits which were appropriate after their baptism (Acts 2:42).

## Rebaptism and Different Baptisms

We can now tie together the idea of repentance as a turning to learn, baptism as an enrollment in a school to learn from the Messiah, and the rebaptisms which are otherwise so perplexing, for rebaptism raises the question: How is Christian baptism related to the baptisms of John the Baptist?

John's gospel tells us that several disciples of John the Baptist left him to follow Jesus (John 1:35-41). We are also told that before John was put in prison, baptisms were being performed both among those who wanted to follow John the Baptist and among those who followed Jesus (John 3:22-24). There is the third suggestion that John's disciples were upset that the number of people becoming disciples of Jesus was greater than the number joining their own group. John the Baptist humbly tells them that this is the way it should be, since "he must increase, but I must decrease" (John 3:26-30).

It has already been noted that, according to John's gospel, baptism was the means used to make disciples both in John's circle of disciples and among the disciples of Jesus. "When the Lord knew that the Pharisees had heard that Jesus was making and baptizing more disciples than John (although Jesus himself did not baptize, but only his disciples), he left Judea" (John 4:1-3). The words in parenthesis inform us that presumably after the first one or two disciples had been baptized the actual rite could be performed by those already in the circle, rather than by the teacher himself. Paul makes a similar point when he admits that though he did perform one or two baptisms in Corinth, most of the actual baptizing was performed by others. (1 Cor. 1:13-17).

Scholars all agree that John the Baptist baptized

followers and that there were Christian baptisms after the day of Pentecost. Those who question the historical accuracy of John's gospel usually assume that Jesus did not baptize, and the texts we have quoted were inserted for polemical reasons. The reason given is that there is no statement in any of the three synoptic Gospels that Jesus baptized or made disciples by baptism. Our main source of information about the first Christian baptisms is the book of Acts. Since Luke is assumed to be the author of both the Gospels of Luke and Acts, why does he not mention baptisms by Jesus if in fact such baptisms took place?

Those scholars who accept the fact that perhaps there were baptisms in the circle of Jesus' disciples have a further problem about the relationship of any of Jesus' baptisms to John's baptisms, and the relationship of both of these to the baptisms after Pentecost. There seem to be six possibilities, as shown in the table on page 57.

If our only sources are the Gospel of Luke and the book of Acts, can we settle which of these six possibilities was in the author's mind?

The first two possibilities are easily dispensed with, if only from the decisive case of the rebaptisms in Ephesus: "He found some disciples. And he said to them, 'Did you receive the Holy Spirit when you believed?' And they said, 'No, we have never even heard that there is a Holy Spirit.' And he said, 'Into what then were you baptized?' They said, 'Into John's baptism.' And Paul said, 'John baptized with the baptism of repentance, telling the people to believe in the one who was to come after him, that is, Jesus.' On hearing this they were baptized in the name of the Lord Jesus" (Acts 19:1-5). We have alrady noted that Luke begins the book of Acts with a statement that he is writing a continuation of what Jesus began to do and to teach. But, in his gospel he has already indicated that Jesus' lifestyle and teaching were radically different from John's. "They said to him, 'The disciples of John fast often and offer

|  |  | John | Jesus | Acts |
|---|---|---|---|---|
| 1 | Jesus did not baptize, and the Acts baptisms were a continuation of John's baptism | B | — | B=A |
| 2 | Jesus' baptism and the Acts baptisms were the same as John's baptism | B | B=C | B=C=A |
| 3 | Jesus continued the same baptism as John's but the Acts baptisms were a new development different from both | B | B=C | A |
| 4 | Jesus' baptism was different from John's, and the Acts baptisms were a new development different from both | B | C | A |
| 5 | Jesus did not baptize, and the Acts baptisms were a new development different from John's baptism | B | — | A |
| 6 | Jesus' baptism was different from John's baptisms, and the Acts baptisms were a continuation of Jesus' baptism | B | C | C=A |

In this chart, "B" stands for John's baptism; "C" stands for Christ's baptism—a blank indicates that Luke does not want us to believe that Jesus baptized, "A" stands for the baptisms in the book of Acts. An equal sign (=) indicates that for the author of Luke-Acts the two kinds of baptism are equivalent, similar, or have the same purpose. The lack of an equal sign indicates that, for Luke, the baptisms are viewed as different or discontinuous.

prayers, and so do the disciples of the Pharisees, but yours eat and drink' " (Luke 5:33). From the parable that follows it is clear that the new wine of Jesus' teaching did not and could not fit the teaching of the Pharisee and Baptist groups of disciples (Luke 5:36-37). When the two disciples of John are sent to inquire if Jesus is the Coming One, Jesus tells them to report back his deeds and the preaching of good news to the poor (Luke 7:18-23).

Evidently Luke wants to portray Jesus as doing works and preaching a gospel of which John knew nothing. Jesus then goes on to explain that although John is a great prophet, the least in the Kingdom of God is greater than he (Luke 7:24-28). The two kinds of ministry are quite different. For example, John is an ascetic, but Jesus eats and drinks with tax collectors and sinners (Luke 7:33-34). If the disciples in Jesus' school are to be taught along such different lines, then obviously the baptisms of John and Christian baptism are performed with different purposes in mind.

Although the Ephesus rebaptisms are dealt with under our third possibility, the arguments which showed the total difference in ministry suggested by Luke are sufficient in this case also. In addition, we have the problem of explaining a completely new kind of baptism invented by the early churches, which had no similarity to the previous baptisms. If Luke had wanted to show that the early church baptisms were different from Jesus' baptisms, at least he would have had to mention Jesus' baptisms and to indicate on what new principle the baptisms in Acts were administered.

The fourth possibility gives full weight to the radical difference suggested by Luke between John's ministry and Jesus' ministry. But it shares with the third possibility the difficulty that if Jesus baptized, and the Acts baptisms were on a different principle, then surely Luke would have indicated this. Why begin the Acts narrative with the statement that Luke was about to describe a continuation of what Jesus had begun to do and teach, if in fact the new baptisms were meant to function in a totally different way?

We are therefore left with two possibilities: either Luke meant to indicate that Jesus did not baptize, and the Acts baptisms were a new development different from John's baptisms, or Jesus' baptism was different from John and the baptisms in the book of Acts were a continuation of his ministry.

While possibility five solves some problems, it raises others. If Luke was suggesting that Jesus and his disciples never baptized, how then can he explain the origin of Christian baptism? The book of Acts begins with a strong statement of continuity. "In the first book, O Theophilus, I have dealt with all that Jesus began to do and teach". In his gospel, Luke had already stated that Jesus had "a great crowd of disciples" (Luke 6:17). Presumably there was some method used to enroll these, and if baptism was not used, what other method of enrollment did Jesus use? And if another method of enrollment was used, why was a new Christian baptism invented to enroll disciples for a purpose quite different from John the Baptist's school of disciples? Would those previously enrolled as Jesus' disciples now need the baptism which they had never had? When, for example, were Jesus' twelve apostles baptized, on such a hypothesis?

## The Acts Baptisms as a Continuation of Jesus' Baptisms

Our sixth option has a beautiful simplicity and elegance. The first and last verses of the book of Acts, and all that come between, suggest the continuity of Jesus' ministry. Having been anointed by the Spirit, Jesus enrolled disciples by baptism and taught them. In turn, when anointed by the Spirit, the disciples continued Jesus' work of baptizing and teaching throughout the world.

Our interpretation would then explain why Paul rebaptized the disciples of John in Ephesus. Paul expressly asked them "Into what then were you baptized?" because he was puzzled as to how they could be disciples without the Spirit. When they said they were baptized "into John's baptism," Paul explained that John's baptism, or school of disciples, was merely to teach concerning the one who was to come later, namely Jesus. Obviously, therefore, they should be baptized again, but this time into (*eis*) the name of the Lord Jesus. Presumably they immediately joined the new Christian school in Ephesus and began their life in the Spirit (Acts 19:1-7).

The model also suggests a possible interpretation for

the baptism of Jesus by John the Baptist. Mark gives us no explanation for the baptism of Jesus, nor does Luke. Matthew's gospel states that John the Baptist objected "I need to be baptized by you, and do you come to me?" On our model this would mean that John felt he ought to become Jesus' disciple; how could the voice that merely prepared the way function as the teacher of the Lord? But Jesus answered, "Let it be so now; for thus it is fitting for us to fulfill all righteousness" (Matt. 3:14, 15). Could this be an echo of the truth behind Paul's teaching that Jesus "was born of woman, born under the law, to redeem those who were under the law" (Gal. 4:4)? The suggestion would imply that Jesus, having been raised by Mary, and taught as a child according to Jewish law, then completed his training as man by enrolling himself as a learner from the last of the Old Testament prophets. But instead of being taught by John, he was immediately led away by the Holy Spirit to be prepared for his ministry. Only then did he begin to function as a rabbi to enroll his own disciples.

## Counting the Cost

I have argued that in both John the Baptist's baptisms and in the baptisms into Jesus' circle of disciples before and after Pentecost the meaning of the word "repentance" means a turning to learn about or from the Messiah. However, the lifestyle taught after baptism is quite different among Jesus' disciples when compared with John the Baptist's ascetic, old covenant ministry.

Having said all this, we may still have the gut feeling that repentance somehow includes an element of contrition and commitment to costly service. Consider the rich young ruler (Luke 18:18). He was told, "Sell all that you have and distribute to the poor, and you will have treasure in heaven, and come follow me." Based on this text and the practice of Christian communism in the book of Acts, some sects have required a selling of all possessions in order to join one of their groups. Even those who do not go that far claim that, just as the rich young ruler had to face his own kind of costly repentance, all candidates for baptism must have been faced with the cost of discipleship.

As we have already seen, it would be impossible to check how many of the three thousand on the day of Pentecost were rich, and whether they had actually sold their possessions, *before* being baptized. My suggestion would be that the cost of wholehearted, total commitment should indeed by presented in the church, but the timing is important. It should not be emphasized until the Christian disciple has received sufficient teaching. In the school analogy, the cost of graduate and Ph.D. studies need not be mentioned as the child enters kindergarten.

Looking at the text more carefully we find that the young man already seemed to be a disciple of Jesus, since he called him "good teacher." In our model he would already have been baptized into the circle of Jesus' learners. There is also the suggestion that he had already learned much, and progressed to the point where "only one thing" was still lacking. Perhaps, having received many months of basic teaching, he now hoped to travel around on a full-time basis as a member of Jesus' preaching band. He would have needed the reminder that "foxes have holes and birds have nests," but missionaries of the gospel must not expect a bed for the night. Similarly, the injunction "leave the dead to bury their own dead" was spoken to a man who was invited to "follow me" (Luke 9:59-60).

We have already noted Luke's version of the parable of the church's banquet. Many are invited, but many of those who could be expected to come make trivial excuses. Since there is still room "the poor and the maimed and blind and lame" are to be brought in, and if that does not fill the church others are to be compelled to come in from "the

highways and hedges" (Luke 14:15-24). This parable
serves to justify an open admission policy at the point of
baptism. Repentance before admission is no more than
accepting the invitation by turning to come in.

The counting the cost that comes later is to be looked for
among the baptized. Having received freely, having
tasted the grace of God, having discovered the resources
available to all Christians, we then come to decide our
response. "Here we offer and present unto thee, O Lord,
ourselves, our souls and bodies" are words spoken by those
who have already taken communion."[9] Luke immediately
follows the open admission policy of the banquet parable
with sayings about bearing the cross, counting the cost
before building a tower, and a king who wonders if he can
win against severe odds. The conclusion is "whoever of
you does not renounce all that he has cannot be my disciple" (Luke 14:25-33). This final verse could be used as a
requirement for repentance before baptism, but what
church has ever been so consistently rigorous? Admittedly
Luke uses the word "disciple," but the context immediately after the parable of the banquet indicates that this
is not cost-counting *before* baptism.[10]

We should all take seriously the costly response that is
implicit in discipleship. In that sense we cannot learn in
the school of Jesus without sooner or later facing the cost.
Enrolling in the beginners' class at a mountain climbers'
school may eventually lead to counting the cost of an
Everest expedition, but the principle of learning is "one
thing at a time." Luke's point is that admission for beginners is incredibly wide open to all and sundry, but cost
counting is inescapable. A wilderness survival school
may be open to any who care to enroll. They cannot possibly understand, much less face, what they will, after some
training, be called upon to do. But by the time they are
invited to undertake the rigorous solo segment of the
program, they will already have received the preparation

needed to face it, succeed in it, and enjoy it.

As any serious follower of Jesus knows, even if he counted the cost before baptism, there are further calls to commitment, self-denial, and cross bearing (Luke 14:25-33). If all the cost were set out before we received the love and help and spiritual power, who among us would ever have the courage or commitment to begin? The parable of the sower warns us that wealth will totally choke out some of the seed in the Kingdom, and in his aside about the rich young ruler, Jesus certainly warns that wealth is a tough handicap.[11] But what we cannot do is refuse baptism and teaching by the Holy Spirit to a wealthy person just because he has not yet repented in the sense of being ready, there and then, to give up all he owns.

In the final chapters of this book we will consider the teaching program needed in the churches after baptism. In the Old Testament the priests often failed to teach God's law, and similarly Christian churches have often degenerated into a perpetuation of ignorant darkness. In such cases the fruits of repentance rarely appear. Where the Word of God is taught and applied we inevitably see among the baptized the beautiful fruits of penitence and contrition, followed by amendment of life. But such fruits take time.[12] They cannot be forced by misguided inquiry as to counting the cost, penitence, and assurance of perseverance before baptism. If turning is taught, that is sufficient, and that is what repentance means in connection with baptism. The fruits of repentance, including penitence and dedication, will follow later.

**Questions for Study and Discussion**

1   The author claims that contrition, or deep sorrow for sin (sackcloth-and-ashes repentance) is a comparatively late fruit in a Christian's life. Read the prophet's experience in Isa. 6:1-8. Can you identify when *you* first experienced such a sense of total unworthiness?

2   Think of individuals you have known who have turned (repented

in the third sense) to learn from other ways or sects.
3  List some people or families you know who have turned to begin
   learning in Christian churches.
4  In your own case, how much of the cost of Christian service was
   made known before you began learning? Would you have begun if
   you had known all that was involved?
5  What needs to be faced before enrolling in, for example, a ski school,
   an art school, a *cursillo* (week-end course of intensive instruction
   common in Roman Catholic and other churches)? What about
   enrolling children in a kindergarten, in Cubs or Brownies, in a
   sailing camp? What cost has to be counted, by whom, and at what
   point? Is counting the cost really a condition of enrolling?

## Prayer

*"Thank you, O God, for enrolling me in the school of Jesus' disciples. I
am beginning to see some of the cost. Strengthen me to tackle future
tough assignments in your kingdom."*

## Footnotes

[1] See also Exod. 32:14; 1 Sam. 15:11, 35; Jer. 4:28.

[2] In Jonah chapter 3 the people engage in the "sackcloth" sense of repentance, at which
point God "repented of the evil which he had said he would do to them," which is an
example of the second or "regret" sense.

[3] See Matt. 21:29, 32, where, in each case, the translation should read "changed his
(their) mind". (See also Matt. 27:3; 2 Cor. 7:8; Heb. 7:21.)

[4] David Pawson and Colin Buchanan, *Infant Baptism Under Cross-Examination*, [Grove
Booklet No. 24] Bramcote, Notts.: Grove Books, p. 16 and p. 18, note 3.

[5] The meaning of the Greek word translated "worthy" (*axios*) is "in keeping with." Arndt
and Gingrich compare the translation "fruit in keeping with your repentance" with such
uses as "fruit which corresponds to what he gave us," and "deeds corresponding to the
words" (*A Greek-English Lexicon of the New Testament and Other Early Christian
Literature*, 1957, p. 77 under meaning 1.b.).

[6] The word "worthy" (*axios*) here is the same, and used in the same way as in John's
preaching in Acts 26:20 and in Luke 3:8.

[7] We often forget that all the epistles of the New Testament were written to people who
were already baptized. There is no hint that any practical or moral teaching had been
accepted and acted upon before baptism.

[8] In *The Apostolic Preaching and its Development*, (1936), C. H. Dodd distinguished
between proclamation or heralding (*kerugma*) and teaching (*didache*). The problem was
to draw a hard line between these in terms of content. What can be distinguished clearly
is the function of *heralding* or *announcing the existence of a school* of the Holy Spirit
from the function of *being a teacher in the school*. An apostle engaged in church planting
had to be able to do both.

[9] Anglican Book of Common Prayer, Rite of Holy Communion.

[10] Similarly, the call to costly service given in conferences such as the Keswick movement
is not a requirement for baptism, much less for earning one's salvation. It is a call to
disciples who have already learned enough of the richness and grace of God to respond
with gratitude.

[11] Luke changes the future tense used in Mark's gospel to "with what difficulty those having possessions *are* entering the Kingdom of God" (Luke 18:24). He could see in the early churches how hard it was for the rich to change their lifestyle and attitudes, but the epistles indicate that rich people were certainly an integral part of the church community (James 1:9-11; 2:1-7; 5:1-6).

[12] This is not to deny that in some cases deep penitence will precede baptism, and Peter certainly pointed out the sin of Jerusalem as a motive for enrolling to learn (Acts 2:23). What does not fit the New Testament evidence is a model that *requires the examination* of sufficient penitence, contrition, or commitment to sacrificial service before baptism.

# Faith

*"Men, what must I do to be
saved?" And they said,
"Believe in the Lord Jesus Christ
and you will be saved and your
household." . . . and he was baptized
at once with all his family
(Acts 16:30-33).*

# 5

IN THE PREVIOUS CHAPTER WE DISTINGUISHED three
meanings of the word "repentance," arguing that sackcloth-and-ashes penitence was certainly not a prerequisite for the immediate baptisms in the New Testament. The
natural sense of the word was that there must be a *turning*
to enroll oneself, and one's family where possible, to begin
learning about Jesus Christ in a school of the Holy Spirit
or local church.

Similarly we need to clarify the words "faith" and "believing." Theologians all agree that there is a close connection between faith and baptism. Baptists insist that
faith must precede baptism, and since children cannot
have faith, only adults should be baptized. Other churches
require some profession of faith on the part of parents or
godparents. Another interpretation is that infant bap-

tism, in some sense, looks forward to, and is completed in, adult faith. But, in any case, these interpretations all stress that faith, baptism, and justification by faith are closely related. I want to argue that despite their close relationship, the exact manner in which the connection is made between them only appears clearly when we distinguish some different meanings of the verb "believe" and the related noun "faith."

The story of the Philippian jailer has already been used to illustrate the point that the baptisms recorded in the New Testament appear to have taken place immediately, without a probationary period. Nor was there time to observe the fruits of repentance, since of course fruits take time to appear. We are, however, informed that the jailer was told to "believe in the Lord Jesus." Based on this, and other references to faith, Baptist theologians argue that nobody can be a candidate for baptism unless he first has believed. They therefore suppose that all the members of the jailer's household must have heard Paul's preaching, understood the gospel, and believed. They quote the words "And they spoke the word of the Lord to him and to all that were in his house," which precede the narrative of the actual baptism. According to one interpretation we must assume that Paul and Silas took time to check the genuineness of the faith of each individual in the house before baptizing him. Another view is that at least the candidates for baptism made a credible profession of faith.

A further assumption, made in most discussions of baptism, is that the faith of the jailer and his household before baptism was the same as the justifying faith spoken of by Paul in his Epistle to the Romans. The implied sequence is that the faith in Jesus required for baptism is justifying faith; justifying faith saves us, and baptism is then a sign, or seal, or confession of that faith, expressed publicly before God and before the people in the congregation. On the Baptist model of baptism, it is this sequence of justifying faith, salvation, and public confession, preferably in believers' baptism by immersion, which makes a person a Christian.

Many of those who practice infant baptism have the nagging feeling that adult baptism, or rather baptism *after* faith, is the norm. Some Anglican theologians have been suggesting that it would be better to discourage infant baptisms and move towards baptism after a clear profession of faith. Others insist that if infants are to be baptized, then we should make sure that the parents, or at least the godparents, have justifying faith. Evangelical preachers in many churches that practice infant baptism use language that suggests that the child will only become a real Christian when, one day, he makes a clearly informed decision of faith, followed by some act of public confession in confirmation or some other occasion. In this connection they quote the text "man believes with his heart and so is justified, and confesses with his lips and so is saved" (Rom. 10:10). All these evangelical interpretations take it for granted that the faith connected with baptism is justifying faith.

Now there are some obvious difficulties in this facile assumption. We have noted that the parable of the sower implies that fruitful faith can only be discerned over a period of time. How then could fruitful faith be discerned if baptisms are to be immediate? And if justifying faith is the same as fruitful faith, how can it possibly be present before baptism? In Luke's account of the parable, the second class of person, sown in shallow ground, who shrivels up under trouble or persecution, is described as believing "for a while." When such failure of faith occurs the usual evangelical interpretation is that the person never had genuine faith in the first place. But this admission grants the point that genuine faith cannot be discerned at the point of baptism. The gospel specifies the touchstone of genuineness: "those who, hearing the word, hold it fast in an honest and good heart, and bring forth fruit with patience" (Luke 8:15). Different meanings of the word faith, and qualities of faith, need to be clearly distinguished. After all, "even the demons believe and shudder" (James 2:19).

## Believing in a School

Let us consider, for example, the many meanings of the words "faith" and "believe" in the ordinary language we use in connection with enrollment. Imagine that a new school has opened in your community. The unique feature of this school is that it offers education for whole families, and will take in anyone, of any age or intellectual capacity, with a view to developing their potential to the full. A man reads about the project in a newspaper article and has faith that the school could help his retarded boy, and perhaps himself too. Another says, "I have great faith in the principal, but I want to wait a bit before enrolling my child." Are these two kinds of faith the same? And what if a child presses her parents to enroll her because she has a good friend who attends? Does she have faith? And if she does not, would she be enrolled? Perhaps you say "she believes she would see more of her friend," but that is not faith in the school. What if someone says, "I have great faith in this school," but does nothing about enrolling his family? Would we say his faith was defective, or non-existent? We can see many possible uses of the word "believe" and "faith" in deciding, or not deciding, to enroll oneself or one's family in such a school.

Now, having enrolled, or having been enrolled in a school or similar institution, how do we use the word "faith"? We understand what is meant by "he's lost faith in the school" in answer to the question "why did he quit?" But we don't at that point discuss whether his faith in the school was genuine in the first place. We can also say "he has lost faith in the school" although he is still attending. Would it be possible to have lost faith in a school, yet later discover that you had gained immense benefits from it? And what of the one who says "I believe in the school for my children, but I refuse to attend myself"? It is appropriate to say of an enthusiastic advocate "he has tremendous faith in the school," and yet we could also say of the same man "he does not believe the school can survive" (e.g. for financial reasons). Then there is the person who has quit, with his family, because he is miffed over some personal matter, but secretly wishes he could rejoin. Has he lost faith, has he had his faith shaken, or does he still have a real faith, although missing the school's benefits?

Anyone who has learned to speak English knows how to use the words "faith" and "believing" in all these complex variations. What we cannot do is to assume that there is some quality, or substance, or emotion that is consistently the same in each case, and it can be called "faith." If we use the words relating to faith with such subtlety in various contexts relating to schools, families, and churches, it is nonsense to assume that the ordinary Greek words for "faith" and "believing" can be used to mean only one particular thing in the New Testament. There is no reason to suppose that faith to be baptized is the same commodity as justifying faith, or faith in God, or in Jesus Christ, or in prayer, or the faith to remove mountains.

The Epistle to the Hebrews distinguishes Moses' faith in leading the people out of Egypt (Heb. 11:27) from the kind of faith lacking in the people which prevented them from entering into the Promised Land (Heb. 3:12-19). He explains that the baptized Christians whom he is addressing could also fail to enter God's rest by unbelief (Heb. 3:19-4:12). We must therefore further distinguish the faith of the one who decides to be baptized with his family from the faith later required by an individual to avoid shrinking back, drifting away from the church or committing apostasy (Heb. 2:1; 6:6; 10:39).

We therefore have one set of uses for the words "faith" and "believing" in connection with the initial joining of the school. We can say "he believed in Jesus Christ, and he was baptized," or "in that town many came to have faith in Christ," or "they turned from faith in other teachers or religions and became Christians." In such cases the meaning is that people believed that Jesus was God's appointed teacher, or at least that he was worth learning from, and they enrolled by baptism to learn from him in the church. Next we distinguish another set of terms connected with justification, and we will argue that justification by faith, or living by faith as opposed to trusting in one's own works, is the main lesson to be learned in the school of Christ after baptism, and it has to be continually relearned in relation to every temptation throughout our Christian lives.

## Faith and Justification

I hope we have said enough to weaken the pervasive idea that faith is a particular commodity, or quality, or emotion, which must exist before baptism. But then, have we not proved too much? Is there not a danger of destroying the great Pauline doctrine of justification by faith? I suggest the very opposite. If we make justification by faith so simple that it can be grasped in the few brief minutes before an immediate baptism, or in even a few days of instruction, we make it trivial. The language of justification belongs to a quite different context. If justification by faith is the main lesson to be learned after baptism throughout our Christian lives, we can give the doctrine the breadth and length and height and depth of the Epistle to the Romans.

First of all we should note that when Paul talks of justification *by faith* he is contrasting it with the attempt to be justified *by works*. Forgiveness is never to be obtained by doing good works to make up for, or pay for our sins (Romans 3:20). Forgiveness is based on what Jesus Christ has done, and this has to be accepted as a free gift (3:21-28). The idea that God's love is not earned by our performance is the very first lesson we need in the school of Christ. Many of us need to learn the lesson again and again. Feelings of unworthiness, guilt, and the temptation to wonder whether the likes of us could ever be accepted, let alone loved by God, continue with us to our deathbeds.

Justification is therefore a principle that needs to be taught constantly throughout our Christian lives. Paul had to teach it by letter to the Romans, who had been baptized long before. Justification by faith is not something one can grasp suddenly once for all. Whenever he is assaulted by guilt or shame, or paralyzed into ineffectiveness, the most mature Christian needs to be reminded by others in the school, or by his own reading of the Scriptures, that forgiveness and all of God's love is given freely. Admittedly, some people may grasp something of the idea of justification before baptism, but it is not the grasp of doctrine that saves. Children may or may not understand that they will be loved regardless of how good they are, but whether they know or don't know it, they will not be able to verbalize in any logical way till very much later how unconditional love differs from earned love. And of course many adopted children feel that love has to be earned by performance long after they have joined a loving family. In actual fact it is impossible to learn unconditional love until you have experienced and tested it over a considerable period of time. How then can we make an intellectual understanding of justification by faith a condition of entering the school of Christ?

Faith is the foundational principle by which we live the Christian life. We need faith as opposed to accepting the burden of our guilt. We trust the Holy Spirit as opposed to trusting our own wisdom. We trust God to work all things together for good even when things go badly by our standards. We trust God to work in us the fruit of the Spirit as opposed to the works of the flesh. We have faith in the eventual triumph of Christ, and we trust him in the hour of death to take us through the dark valley to a glorious resurrection. Is all this faith to be required before baptism? Evidently not, otherwise the epistles would not have been written to baptized Christians. The fact is that the school of Christ has to be the vehicle of the Holy Spirit to teach the application of simple childlike faith to every area of our lives, and that teaching begins with baptism. In the New Testament baptism is never postponed for an individual until a certain amount of faith, or evidence of successful living by faith, can be observed in him.

**Saving Faith**
What then of saving faith? The idea very easily suggests that somehow faith is a work that *we* perform. We must keep reminding ourselves that it is Christ alone who saves us through his death and resurrection and the giving of the Holy Spirit for every need of the Christian life. That means that we need to be careful of the languge we use. We can say "he believed in Jesus Christ and was baptized with his family" which would be a historical fact. We cannot say "he was saved by faith" as if it were something that happened once and for all, in the past. Are we to imagine an amount of faith, or a quality of faith, or an act of faith, or feeling of faith, that occurred once and guar-antees a place in heaven regardless of one's freedom in the future? And even if there were such a once-for-all faith deep in the heart of any person we have already shown from many angles that it could not be checked before an immediate baptism.

New Testament faith is a direction of trust, an abiding heart-confidence like Abraham's, not a measurable grasp of the intellect. The idea of saving faith is derived from verses such as "man believes with his heart and so is justified, and he confesses with his lips and so is saved" (Romans 10:10). This certainly means that if our heart is looking to God we have no need to worry about adequate performance in order to be justified. I don't think the verse requires us to specify how much intelligent understanding of the mystery of the atonement will save us. If intelligent understanding were specified, what would we say of little children, or the retarded? Nor does confession with the lips need to be limited to one act of confession at a particular time.

Am I then denying that we can be assured of forgiveness, acceptance by a loving God, our place in the City of God in heaven? Certainly not. If our hearts look to God we can be totally sure that God knows us to the core, and still loves us. As we become conscious of our own sinfulness and inability to love God as we ought, we should understand that the death of Jesus Christ on the cross more than takes care of our pardon. His blood is sufficient to cover our darkest sin. His resurrection has the power to take us with him through death, and transform us all into the renewed body, mind, and spirit that we need to have in heaven. We can therefore be absolutely sure that nothing can separate us from the love of God and that we already have eternal life. Justification is therefore a fact of God's love for us, regardless of whether we understand it, and of course most of us understand it inadequately. It is good to enter into the mystery of how we are loved, and accepted, and justified, but we are unlikely to have more than an inkling of its glory when we begin our discipleship.

### The Unbaptized
If justification by faith is usually learned throughout our discipleship after baptism, what then of the unbaptized?

Is both faith and the denial of faith impossible to them? Again we remind ourselves of the purpose of our school. The function of registration is not to guarantee places in heaven. Nor is it to consign those who do not register to hell. Its one purpose is to introduce them to teaching by the Holy Spirit in the learning community which we call the church. The main lesson to be learned in the school is justification by faith, but we do not say that it would be impossible to learn this or any other lesson from God in some other way. Although the Old Testament tells us that Israel is God's chosen people, and that it is among them that he intends to teach his ways, no dogma holds that justifying faith is impossible among the uncircumcised. Paul expressly tells us that Abraham was justified by faith long before his circumcision (Rom. 4:9-11). Nor does the New Testament say that the unbaptized will go to hell.[1] Although the Christian church, and no other institution, is appointed by God to teach justification by faith in Christ, it would be ridiculous to claim that nobody outside the church can learn of God by other means.

As we have seen, the New Testament is clear that no one can be ultimately saved except through the death and resurrection of Jesus Christ. He himself said, "no one comes to the Father, but by me" (John 14:6). But it is important to add that the New Testament does not say that conscious understanding of *how* Jesus died and rose again is required to come to the Father. Abraham was justified by faith, and in fact his faith is a paradigm of faith, but he certainly did not understand how the Messiah would eventually come and save him. Thus we cannot rule out the possibility that others before and after Abraham, and in other countries, have indeed exercised a true faith and found access to God as Father without understanding the exact means of their salvation through Christ. In any case, we have to admit that multitudes of children, the mentally deficient, and senile persons will be saved through Jesus Christ without an intellectual understanding of the cross. We are saved through Christ, not by an intellectual grasp of what he did for us.

This brings us back to the focal point of this chapter. The faith that precedes baptism is faith to begin learning—with one's family in a local church, or school of the Holy Spirit. Justification is the main topic to be learned in the school. When the idea of justification is grasped it should be expressed with our lips, both in praise and thanksgiving to God, and in witness to others. We are justified, not by a single decision of faith but by faith itself, which is an attitude, a direction of looking, a way of walking like Abraham. And it is that way of walking which is what discipleship is all about. It obviously cannot be required before baptism.

## Faith and the Creed

What then of reciting and professing the Creed? We will be taking up in a later chapter the practical questions of what should be understood before baptism. Meanwhile it should be obvious that we cannot require an intellectual grasp of every article in the Creed from retarded and or simple-minded people, and they should be welcomed in any loving school of the Holy Spirit. Any of us who have spent a lifetime struggling to grasp the meaning of various articles of the Creed could never demand a comprehensive understanding of even the most intelligent new disciple. What, then, are we doing in demanding assent to this formidable statement of complex theological doctrines? I suggest that the Creed is more a syllabus than a test. Expressed within it are the main items to be learned after baptism, with their implications in the life of faith. When we enroll in a university course we are given an outline of what the professor intends to teach us. We assent to being taught the whole course by the act of enrolling. Only after months of instruction is it feasible to ask how much we have actually mastered.

So it is with the Creed. If it is to be mastered before baptism, then baptisms cannot be immediate, and we have seen that that would be a denial of New Testament practice. Recited and assented to in the baptismal service, it is a useful reminder that baptism is not an end but a beginning in the school of the disciples of Jesus, and there is much to be learned.

## Is Faith Decisional or Directional?

John 3:16 is the favorite verse in the Bible. It is called the gospel in a nutshell, and most people assume that its meaning is obvious. The difficulty is that the meaning of the word "believes" is governed by the church model that influences us. Many evangelical churches interpret the verse in a decisional way: "God so loved the world that he gave his only son that whoever makes a decision for him should not perish but have eternal life." In India I knew missionaries who genuinely believed that unless the millions of people around them heard the gospel and made a decision to accept Jesus Christ they were condemned to hell. But is this what the writer of the Gospel had in mind?

In the verses that follow immediately after our text faith is exactly defined as *loving the light.* Just as plants are light-loving, and instinctively turn towards light, so believers love and turn towards the light of God. Unbelievers hate it. Man's reaction to the light of God is the judgment (*krisis*): "This is the judgment, that the light has come into the world, and men loved darkness rather than light, because their deeds were evil. For every one who does evil hates the light, and does not come to the light, lest his deeds should be exposed. But he who does what is true comes to the light, that it may be clearly seen that his deeds have been wrought in God" (John 3:19-21). Now on this interpretation of faith the Old Testament believers, such as Abraham, Moses, and David, obviously loved the light of God. Since Jesus is the light made flesh (John 1:4-18) all light-lovers will love him.

John's gospel therefore views faith as directional, not as a decisional, cerebral act. In *The Great Divorce*, C. S. Lewis gives us an extended allegory of this kind of faith. Hell is inevitable only for those who would find the light of heaven unbearable. Presumably only God can know who are the light-lovers, or believers, in this sense.

If we assume that saving faith in John 3:16 is decisional, then we will interpret Paul's teaching of justification by faith in a similar way. "Those who make a decision for Christ are justified." If, on the other hand, Paul had the same directional view of faith as John's gospel, then those who are justified are the ones who love the light of God. Since a large part of Paul's argument is based on Abraham's faith it seems very hard to believe that Abraham was justified by making a decision to accept Christ as his personal Savior.

What then of the categorical statement in John's gospel, "I am the way, and the truth, and the life; no one comes to the Father but by me" (John 14:6)? Many evangelical churches assume that this means that no one can be in heaven unless they hear, understand, and accept the death of Jesus Christ to save them. But does this not mean that children, retarded and senile persons, and all the heathen will be in hell? Such churches naturally shrink from following their line of logic to the bitter end. But there again we can be categorical in saying that no one will be in heaven unless he loves it. We can also be quite categorical in saying that anyone in heaven, whether infant or retarded, whether responsible or senile, whether before or after the life of Christ, will discover that he is there only by virtue of the death and resurrection of Jesus. What the New Testament never says is that only people who grasp *cerebrally* what Jesus has done, and accept it by an informed decision of faith will be in heaven. This means that justification is by faith, not by a decision of faith, in any cerebral or intellectual sense.

The Bible is quite clear that there are two ultimate destinies for every person who has ever lived, or will live in our world. There is no trace of universalism, which suggests that God will somehow force everyone to love him willy-nilly. It is true that God is not willing to let anyone perish, but our moral nature requires freedom. The freedom is to love the light, which is God the Trinity of love and perfection, but that freedom also permits us to love the darkness.

We are familiar with the idea of plants loving the light; they will turn and stretch out their leaves to grow toward the light from a dark part of the room. What if there were also darkness-loving plants? If we placed them near the light, they would shrink away and seek to hide in the darkness. There would then be two kinds of plants, light-loving and darkness-loving. That is the imagery of John 3:16-21. All of humanity is one or the other. The difference is that plants are not free to choose. Not only are we free to love the light of God, as fully revealed in Jesus Christ, but we are also free to prefer the darkness that Satan himself prefers. In some cases people love God from their earliest days. In others, after loving the darkness for many years, or being double-minded for some time, there is a conversion from darkness to light. The conversion may be preceded by intense struggle, and God may even force the doubter down into further darkness before he sees the real implications of what darkness means. This seems to be the meaning of the three terrible "handing over" passages in Rom. 1:18-32. In other cases, after a period of hypocrisy or superficial religion, there seems to be a deliberate turning away or apostasy into the darkness. Even in such cases God still loves, and hopes, and uses every means to persuade the loved one to turn to the light.

A concern that is often expressed relates to freedom of choice. How can faith be an expression of our ultimate freedom if it does not begin with a decision? All I want to deny is the need for cerebral understanding and decision in a sense that would exclude the retarded, infants, the senile, and all who have never been taught justification by faith. Faith must be a free response to the love of God. As long as we can exclude the intellectual content there is no harm in thinking of such faith as an expression of our choice. I also suspect that faith in the sense of John 3:18-21 need not require a conversion at a point in time. Many who are raised in a loving Christian home can never remember when they did not love the Lord, and John the Baptist was filled with the Holy Spirit from his mother's womb (Luke 1:15).

## Making Decisions

Having insisted that we are justified by faith, not by a decision of faith, there is no denying that faith may be strengthened by making a decision. Some of the greatest preachers have been used to bring people from the faith of a nominal churchgoer to a more vital faith by persuading them to take a first step of faith. This step is variously called accepting Christ, committal to Christ, receiving Jesus into one's heart, and so on. The result of such a step is often that the individual receives assurance of sins forgiven, eternal life, new strength to live as a Christian, and the start of growth in faith and grace. Many can look back to this first step as the effective beginning of their life of faith. If the step is followed by linking up with a caring group of Christians, Bible study, prayer and worship, training in exercising a gift in the church, then the step is marvellously fruitful. However, it is important to recognize that the step is often taken by a person who is already in the school of Christ. Perhaps he went to Sunday School, wandered away from church for some time, and now,

again, begins serious growth and learning. There is no
harm in calling this step "conversion" as long as we realize
that this turning is distinct from the turning when a
family or an individual first begins to learn from Christ.
It is also important to recognize that some people can
hardly identify such a turning point or crisis in their
Christian life; growth and learning have been fairly
steady since childhood. There has been no crisis of turning
away, like the Prodigal Son. In either case, what is important is that each of us is certain, right now, that we love
loving God, and therefore delight in Jesus Christ, what he
has done for us by his death and resurrection, and what he
is doing for us and in us *now* by the Holy Spirit.

## Saving Faith and Solo Flying

We might compare the steps and decisions of faith to
learning to fly. My decision to enroll in a flying school,
or my parents' decision to enroll, is a step of great potential. If my mental reflexes and physical faculties are
functioning normally, I am reasonably enthusiastic, and
if the flying instructors are competent, I am likely to
progress as follows: I receive some preliminary instruction; I may practice some movements in a dummy cockpit
on the ground; then I fly with an instructor in a plane with
dual controls. Now there has to be a step of faith. For the
first time I have to take off alone. I may do this as naturally as a baby duck going into the water, or I may lose
interest for a time, or I may have a long struggle, with
sleepless nights. I might even quit the flying school for
several years before being finally persuaded to resume
instruction and take my first solo flight. I may or may not
need the help of others in taking this key step of faith.
The point is, once I can fly, those early decisions of faith no
longer seem important. My skill in flying does not depend
on my being able to say how I took the first step. I may
record and treasure the date of my first solo flight, or I may

not even remember how I learned. The important thing is that *I can fly.*

Similarly, in the Christian faith, my grasp of justification by faith and living by faith may come naturally, I may experience it after many struggles, I may need a personal counsellor or preacher to make it clear, but the important thing is that I am living by faith now, which was the whole purpose of enrolling in the school of Christ in the first place.

### Three Kinds of Faith in Relation to Baptism

By way of reviewing some different meanings of the words "faith" and "believing" in this chapter, we must distinguish:

*1 Faith to enroll* by baptism, as in the book of Acts. The individual, or the head of the household, decides to enroll himself or herself with a view to beginning to learn from the risen and ascended Lord Jesus Christ by the Holy Spirit.

*2 Faith as a movement toward the light,* as in John 3:18-21 and Heb. 10:38-11:16. This is the kind of faith illustrated by C. S. Lewis in *The Great Divorce.* It distinguishes the lover of light from the lover of darkness. It can exist without intellectual understanding, as in little children, retarded persons, the untaught, etc.

*3 Justification by faith,* as a doctrine to be understood intellectually by those whose hearts are already directed toward God. Obviously the Romans, to whom Paul was writing, were already baptized and so had the faith to enroll (1), and presumably most of them had hearts right with God (2), but they lacked an understanding of salvation as a free gift. If we are to baptize 3,000 new learners on one day, or waken a sleepy household to be baptized before breakfast, we cannot require the demonstration of a clear grasp of justification by faith.

**Questions for Study and Discussion**
1  The author points out a variety of meanings of the words "faith"
   and "believing" in connection with schools and education. List a
   similar variety of meanings in connection with faith in doctors,
   diets, medical drugs, operations, and healing.
2  When did it first dawn on you that God loves you unconditionally?
   How often have you had to relearn this lesson?
3  Using the illustration of the flying school, at what point would you
   say you began flying solo as a Christian? Compare your experience
   with those who say they have loved God from their earliest days,
   or with those who have had an earthshaking adult conversion.
4  What does the author mean by saying "we are justified not by a
   decision of faith, but by faith which is an attitude, a direction of
   looking"? Is your faith decisional or directional?
5  What is the function of the Creed or other statement of faith in
   your own church's baptismal services?

**Prayer:**
*"Thank you, Father, that your love for me is unconditional. Somehow
you have brought me to accept your love, and in that love I am safe. Help
me to share your love with others as I invite them into the family of
your people."*

**Footnotes**
[1] The one text that might suggest that the unbaptized will all be damned is from the
questionable last 12 verses of Mark's gospel, which are not included in Bible versions
that reflect the best texts: "He who believes and is baptized will be saved: but he who
does not believe will be condemned." But even if this text is authentic, or reflects an early
church outlook, the word "condemned" need not necessarily mean exclusion from heaven.

# Regeneration

*He saved us, not because of
deeds done in righteousness, but
in virtue of his own mercy, by the
washing of regeneration and renewal
in the Holy Spirit
(Titus 3:5).*

# 6

---

IN EVANGELICAL THEOLOGY, REGENERATION is usually identified with being "born again." This is taken to mean an experience of conversion and faith, resulting in forgiveness of sin, adoption into the family of God, and the gift of eternal life. Baptists add that this one saving event must precede baptism. Our analysis has highlighted the problem that if New Testament baptisms were immediate, there was no way to check the genuineness of the experience of the baptized. What assurance could there be that the three thousand baptized on the day of Pentecost were all truly regenerate? We find that the New Testament writers mention without surprise how many of the baptized went back from discipleship, apostasized, became false teachers and false prophets. How can those who in due course fail to produce the good fruit of the parable of the sower be viewed as having been saved, born again, or having eternal life?

**Nicodemus—What Kind of a Disciple?**
Our task in this chapter is therefore to consider how the school model of baptism affects an evangelical interpretation of the doctrines of regeneration and the new birth. We begin with the key passage concerning Nicodemus' need to be born again as described in John 3. Nicodemus recognized that Jesus had a right to be a rabbi teaching disciples because he was obviously "a teacher come from God." We argued in earlier chapters that the word "disciple" means a learner, and both John and Jesus used baptism as the means of enrolling their own disciples. What then was Nicodemus' need?

Evidently he was not yet a disciple of Jesus, although he was "the teacher of Israel" (John 3:10, which includes the Greek definite article). Nicodemus was therefore one of the leading rabbis and would presumably have his own circle of disciples. When he came to Jesus by night he hoped to find out what Jesus was teaching which exhibited a spiritual power that he did not have. Jesus' answer was simple. One must be born again "of water and the Spirit." At first Nicodemus took this literally, asking how he could go back into his mother's womb. Or he may have been making a metaphorical allusion to the difficulty facing an old rabbi who must start over again to learn as a disciple. The suggestion, later in John's gospel, is that Joseph of Arimathea was a secret disciple, and "Nicodemus also;" together they took Jesus down from the cross and buried him (John 19:38, 39).

Now, as we use our model of baptism as enrollment into Jesus' school of disciples, a simple explanation emerges. Nicodemus had been taught by the law in the rabbinic schools of Jerusalem. Eventually he had become one of the best known rabbis in the country with his own following of disciples. He recognizes the spiritual power of Jesus' teaching, and realizes that he needs this power himself. Jesus explains that the only way for him to learn is to be baptized with water, to join Jesus' circle of disciples, and be taught in that circle by the Holy Spirit. John suggests later that both Nicodemus and Joseph of Arimathea did, in fact, do that.

On this interpretation the new birth is not a spiritual experience which guarantees a place in heaven. We avoid the dilemma of trying to prove the genuineness of faith before baptism. If Nicodemus was baptized and began to learn from Jesus Christ, he was born again. The invisible wind of the Spirit would begin to affect him in the same way it had affected the less educated Galilean disciples. Whether he would continue to learn or go back, is not at issue. Within the circle of disciples, Nicodemus would grasp the spiritual truths which the law had not given him. He would discover justification by faith, the assurance of being loved as a child of God, the purpose of Jesus' coming and crucifixion, the certainties of forgiveness and eternal life. Thus, his new birth would have great promise. It does not need to be an attainment that can be measured or checked. His baptism and beginning to learn could be immediate, and his instruction would be by the Spirit, from Jesus himself.

### The New Birth
After the Holy Spirit has been poured out in the church to continue Jesus' work of training disciples, the same language of the new birth applies. The question "What shall we do?" which followed Peter's preaching corresponds to the question that Nicodemus had in mind. The procedure is the same. "Be baptized with water, and you will receive the gift of the Spirit." And, in fact, we find that the three thousand were then enrolled for "the apostles' teaching and fellowship" and the full life of worship and prayer in

the Spirit (Acts 2:41, 42).

Peter uses the same language of being born again in his letter to Christians from several regions of Asia Minor. "By his great mercy we have been born anew to a living hope through the resurrection of Jesus Christ from the dead" (1 Pet. 1:3). "You have been born anew, not of perishable seed but of imperishable, through the living and abiding word of God" (1 Pet. 1:23). He then indicates that these are not mature, proven Christians, but new converts. "Like newborn babes, long for the pure spiritual milk, that by it you may grow up to salvation" (1 Pet. 2:2). It is unlikely that there would be any fewer future apostates, false teachers, and false prophets among these "born again" Christians than in Paul's churches. In Peter's second epistle we read "false prophets also arose among the people, just as there will be false teachers among you" (2 Pet. 2:1). Even if the second epistle is much later than the first, it still indicates that first century Christians expected those who had been born again by baptism and life in the Spirit to have spiritual casualties among their number.

### In the Holy Spirit
Once we have freed the idea of being born again from spiritual attainment and assurance of long term continuance in the faith, it then becomes a very appropriate image for beginning to learn by the Holy Spirit. Here, depending on the method used to administer baptism for the children of Christians, we will have two terminologies.

If someone is baptized as a baby as a sign of being enrolled by his family to be taught by the Holy Spirit, but then is either never taught or wanders away from Christian teaching for some time, he needs to be born again. Eventually he may hear the word of an evangelist, or be persuaded by other means, or become concerned to learn. As soon as he begins to study the Bible and finds himself enjoying the teaching and worship of a "live" church or fellowship, we can say he is born again. It is only when people are added to a community where they are well taught, and the gentle wind of the Spirit moves among them, that we can see the evidence of new birth. There may admittedly be some who will turn back, hardening their hearts, and even becoming false teachers of various kinds, but the first experience of fullness of life in the Spirit is appropriately called the new birth. I would suggest that for many who have been blessed through the charismatic movement this is in fact what happened to them. They had previously known some cerebral teaching, had some doctrinal grasp of justification by faith, but then the wind of the Spirit filled their sails and they were moved in a vital and continuous relationship with God.

We must now take the case of churches which practice infant dedication. Obviously they too will want their children to experience the Spirit from their earliest days. If John the Baptist was filled with the Holy Spirit from his mother's womb (Luke 1:15) there is presumably no age that is too young for a child to experience the new birth in that sense. Often, in fact, the children of Christian homes will experience the work of the Spirit, have doubts, struggle to find their own faith, make decisions of various kinds and finally focus their attention on learning seriously from the Spirit among God's people. That is often the point at which baptism is administered among those who practice infant dedication. Now, when the families of Lydia and the Philippian jailer were baptized were the infants baptized, or were they dedicated with a view to a later baptism? As I have already pointed out, it seems to me impossible to prove from Scripture which method was used.

What is essential is that, as soon as the parents are enrolled by baptism, the babes in arms are also introduced to the Holy Spirit through prayer, and family singing, bedtime stories, and in worshipping with God's people. Even if only one parent takes faith seriously, the child is considered "holy" (1 Cor. 7:14). And we have all seen the wind of the Spirit blowing in such homes where the grace of God can get a foothold. If we have to become like little children to enter the kingdom of God, it would seem incongruous to suggest that babes in arms are too young! Nor does the enrollment for teaching, whether by infant baptism or infant dedication, deny the right of children to think for themselves. The freedom to choose requires a thorough knowledge of the alternatives, and nobody has been given the true freedom to reject the Christian faith if they have never been given the chance to learn it.

### Salvation and the Exodus
We now return to the text with which we introduced this chapter. "He saved us ... by the washing of regeneration and renewal in the Holy Spirit" (literally, "renewal of the Holy Spirit," Titus 3:5). The sequence of washing, or baptism, followed by a work of the Holy Spirit, seems to be the same as in Jesus' words to Nicodemus. Possibly the use of the word "regeneration" corresponds to the idea of being born again in John's gospel and in Peter's letter. In Titus there is, however, the added idea of salvation by baptism. But this salvation through baptism cannot be seen as an individual experience guaranteeing eternal life. The Epistle of Jude definitely views salvation as a corporate act: "He who saved a people out of the land of Egypt, afterward destroyed those who did not believe" (Jude 5).

### Corporate Regeneration
When large numbers are baptized almost immediately after hearing a message from God, the individual's quality of faith cannot be checked. And yet on the day of Pentecost

Peter calls on his hearers to "save yourselves from this crooked generation" (Acts 2:40), and the response is that three thousand are baptized. Later in the chapter we read that "the Lord added to their number day by day those who were being saved" (Acts 2:47). If "salvation" does not refer to the eternal destiny of individuals who have a genuine faith, what then can it mean?

We note the connection made by Paul between baptism and the crossing of the Red Sea. "Our fathers were all under the cloud, and all passed through the sea, and all were baptized into Moses in the cloud and in the sea, and all ate the same supernatural food and all drank the same supernatural drink" (1 Cor. 10:1-4). Admittedly the people had to cross the Red Sea as individuals, and in that sense they were baptized into Moses individually. But they also all shared in a corporate, saving act of God. A new people was created by their crossing of the Red Sea. Paul points out that this does not guarantee that they will continue, and it certainly had nothing to do with places in heaven (1 Cor. 10:5). The fact that the first Exodus was viewed as God's salvation of a people out of bondage is frequently referred to in the Old Testament. The idea is picked up in the New Testament in the text we have already quoted: "He who saved a people out of the land of Egypt, afterward destroyed those who did not believe" (Jude 5; Exod. 14:13, 30; 15:2, 13, etc.). Now, in view of the close connection set up by the early church between the Exodus and their New Exodus, should we not suspect that New Testament salvation was viewed in a similar way? Thus baptism into Christ creates a new people, who are saved from sin. The people of the Exodus were to be "a kingdom of priests and a holy nation" (Exod. 19:6), and this language is applied exactly "as is" by Peter to the Church. "You are a chosen race, a royal priesthood, a holy nation, God's own people, that you may declare the wonderful deeds of him who called you out of darkness" (1 Pet.

2:9). Similarly, the language of redemption is taken straight from the Exodus event and applied to the baptized.

In view of all these tight connections I suggest that regeneration is a term that may be applied both to the salvation of the first Exodus and to the New Exodus. When the people had crossed the Red Sea it could be said of them that "they are now regenerate." A new birth had occurred in them as God's people. In the New Testament therefore "the washing of regeneration" had nothing to do with an inward heart change, but rather with what God had done by adding a person to the Church of the Messiah to be taught by the Holy Spirit. The terms "saved" and "salvation" are corporate rather than individualistic. Persons are added either in large groups or as individuals to the body of God's people. I suspect that this was the sense of the phrase, "this child is regenerate" found in Cranmer's Anglican Prayer Book. The very fact that there is a prayer that the baptized will continue among God's people confirms this interpretation.

### Distinction Between Saved and Unsaved—Where?

Is there then no distinction in the Church between spiritual and unspiritual people? Obviously there is, but *not at the point of baptism*. We have noted that the word "Christian" in the New Testament refers to someone who is baptized and under instruction in a local church (Acts 11:26). If apostasy occurs, that person is no longer called a Christian, but rather a disciple who began learning and has now quit. But even among those who are continuing among God's people there are those whose hearts are right with God and those who are children of Belial. At one time Elijah wondered if he was the only true Israelite left, though God could still count seven thousand of them. In the sign of circumcision there is a distinction between outward circumcision and heart circumcision. Paul takes up this same distinction. "He is not a real Jew who is one outwardly ... He is a Jew who is one inwardly, and real circumcision is a matter of the heart, spiritual and not literal" (Rom. 2:28, 29). Similarly, in our churches we may view all the baptized, who are currently learning and worshipping with us, as Christians. We may suspect, like Elijah, that few are true Christians, or real Christians, or heart Christians, or whatever we want to call them. It is an important prophetic task to call people already in our churches to heart baptism, true faith, living by the Spirit, consecration, and renewal. All I have argued is that this distinction between external baptism and heart faith cannot be made at the point of baptism.[1] It may be revealed in time ("by their fruits you shall know them") but ultimately only God knows who are truly his.

### The Effect of Baptism

The efficacy of baptism is a question which has plagued theologians for the past four hundred years. Sacramentalists insist that something is effected by baptism. It is not *just* a symbol or a seal of faith. Evangelicals object that salvation is by faith alone and admit no warrant for making Christians automatically, by a ritual. All would agree that in some cases baptism, functioning as a visible word, does in fact elicit faith, but evangelicals cannot believe that, if faith is lacking, anything has been effected by the rite alone. They are usually uneasy about infant baptism, though some justify it on the charitable assumption that the children of Christians will later come to understand what baptism signifies, and so believe and be saved by the sign. The sacramentalist counters with the many New Testament passages such as Mark 1:3; Luke 3:3; John 13:10; Acts 2:38; 22:16; 1 Cor. 6:11; Eph. 5:26; Titus 3:5; 1 Pet. 3:21; 2 Pet. 2:22 which suggest that grace, and in particular forgiveness, is actually imparted in baptism.

Theologians on either side now admit the force of the
opposite argument. Very few sacramentalists would be
happy about indiscriminate baptisms, as if grace were
imparted in a magical kind of way. From the Baptist side,
the classic modern presentation is Beasley-Murray's *Baptism in the New Testament.* He admits that many of his
conclusions run counter to Baptist "popular tradition." He
is not afraid to insist that the New Testament writers
view baptism "as a symbol with power." He then gives an
astonishing list of graces which are promised, and said to
be granted in baptism. These include forgiveness, cleansing, and release from the power and guilt of sin; union
with Christ's death, resurrection and sonship; membership in the Church, the body of Christ; possession of new
life in the Spirit including spiritual regeneration; deliverance from the evil powers that rule this world and grace
to live according to the will of God; pledge of the resurrection of the body. As a Baptist he seems to grant all that the
sacramentalists have been arguing. For him, baptism is
both instrumental and efficacious.[2]

The Discipleship model of baptism is clearly instrumental. Something is effected by baptism in the New
Testament.[3] There is a change of status in that the baptized are the ones whom the church feels specially responsible to teach. Baptism is instrumental in regeneration in
the same way as crossing the Red Sea was instrumental
in creating a people to be taught by the Law.[4] At the same
time, with this model we have avoided the suggestion of
automatic impartation of grace so abhorrent to evangelicals. By separating the faith to enroll from justification by
faith, which is the main topic of instruction after baptism,
we preserve the emphasis which was so important to
Martin Luther.

As we have noted, there are two main methods of administering the baptism of children from Christian
homes. If infants are baptized, then their baptism corres-

ponds to the baptism into Moses (1 Cor. 10:2) of the babies in arms who went across the Red Sea. If children are baptized later, say at the age of fourteen or after an intelligent profession of faith, then there must be some rite in infancy to signify their enrollment in the school of Christ. In the Jewish *bar mitzvah* a boy takes upon himself the personal responsibility for learning and teaching of the Law. From infancy he is viewed as a Jew and as part of the people who came through the Exodus, and he has already been taught in his Jewish home. His *bar mitzvah* is a sign of the beginning of adult learning. A similar understanding of baptism during one's teens would fit a Discipleship model of the church.

### The Forgiveness of Sins
The next question is whether our model can help us in understanding how baptism can be said to impart the forgiveness of sins (Acts 2:38). This is the chief of the graces that Beasley-Murray admits are granted in baptism. And yet this suggestion of imparting forgiveness has been bitterly opposed by generations of evangelicals. How can the application of water in the name of the Trinity automatically affect a person's eternal destiny? Why should this baptized child have his sins forgiven while the unbaptized go to hell or into limbo?

### Two Models of Baptism
The difficulty is that the discussion of the effects of baptism has polarized around two models, which we have caricatured as follows: A child is born with a heart full of original sin. Baptism washes the sin away and restores the child to pristine purity. After this initial bath all that is needed is washing from time to time by confession and absolution in the sacrament of penance. Any remaining uncleansed sin at death will be purged in purgatory. The other model is that a child is born with a heart full of

original sin. Faith in Jesus Christ as Lord and Savior washes away all past sin and also all future sin. The believer is therefore totally secure in eternal life, and nothing can separate him from the love of God and eventual heaven. Baptism is a sign that this eternal life has already been received, or, in the case of infant baptism, that eternal life is confidently anticipated. While we can agree that both these models are caricatures and no reputable theologian on either side would want to defend them without many qualifications, yet the models have great power in the minds of many people. They reflect the way ordinary Christians in both the sacramentalist and the evangelical camps have visualized the problem.

What then of our school model? The first thing to point out is that both the sacramental and evangelical models, at least in their caricatured form, are obsessed with guaranteeing "places in heaven." How can I be sure my sins are forgiven, and therefore my place in heaven is secure? Our school model has no concern with guaranteeing the eternal state. *All that baptism should guarantee is the opportunity to learn from Jesus Christ by the Holy Spirit among the people of the New Exodus.* After baptism we learn that Jesus Christ has made "a full, perfect, and sufficient sacrifice, oblation, and satisfaction, for the sins of the whole world,"[5] and therefore we need have no fear. God accepts all who come to him, and so we do not require good works to earn our way into heaven.

But does not the New Testament imply that the forgiveness of sins is closely related to baptism, as is stated expressly in our texts from the book of Acts? Yes, it does, but with a very important qualification. The baptismal experience of the forgiveness of sins has nothing to do with an eternal state. This has been sufficiently proved by showing that if baptisms are immediate, fruitful faith cannot be discerned at that point. Also many of the baptized apostasized, becoming false prophets. Baptism was viewed as a washing from sins. But the baptized one could later return to his unwashed state after baptism. Peter admits this: "The sow is washed only to wallow in the mire" (2 Pet. 2:22). The state of being washed and forgiven is the present state of all the baptized, but the condition does not continue where there is apostasy or refusal to live by the Spirit. We therefore need to distinguish this present status of the baptized disciples, who are viewed as forgiven by their fellow Christians, from the eternal state of all who will be in heaven. Of course anyone who is going to be in heaven, and therefore saved by Jesus Christ's death and resurrection, must be forgiven all the past, but most theologians see that happening apart from baptism.[6] Together with evangelical theologians, I refuse to believe that God has appointed baptism as his effective instrument for granting places in heaven by forgiving sin.

## The Status of the Baptized: Forgiven
What then is this status of being viewed as forgiven in the church on earth? The Discipleship model makes clear that neither baptism nor a cerebral decision of faith effects an eternal change in the heart. Our eternal state is governed by whether or not we love and continue to live in the light of God as fully exemplified and incarnated in Jesus Christ (John 3:16-21). We have argued that what is significant is heart direction, not cerebral decision. C. S. Lewis pictures people choosing the Grey City because they freely prefer it. When they take a space trip to view the city of God, they find themselves ill at ease and cannot bear its light and love. Those who are at home in the city are not only forgiven but perfected.[7]

Pointing to the light and the city of God in heaven we have a visible church on earth. In the New Testament, baptism is definitely viewed as imparting membership in this Church. The disciples enrolled by baptism were brought into a community to be taught by the Holy Spirit.

There they were called saints, Christians, holy ones, although it was recognized that some, as apostates, might later decide to leave, and some, as false teachers and prophets, might decide to remain in the church to do the work of Satan.

In the Christian community the disciples learned about the love and forgiveness of God, and they tasted the worship of heaven. They learned to love and be loved. In that circle of love they also learned to forgive. Any who came into the community of the Holy Spirit were accepted, regardless of their past. In the community surrounding Jesus when he was on earth people like Matthew, member of the tax-collecting Mafia, and Mary Magdalene, with her notorious reputaton, were welcomed and viewed as forgiven. In the world around them, people's status depended on performance, as it still does around us. If, and only if, you produce, perform, conform, look beautiful, achieve, give pleasure, you are loved. But as soon as we enter the church our performance, or lack of it, is not counted against us. We are loved unconditionally. In that sense we are accepted, we are washed, we are viewed as forgiven. Baptism must grant us acceptance into that community. No human ritual or decision can impart places in heaven.

## Forgiveness not by Baptism

The story of the healing of the paralytic from Mark is used by both Matthew and Luke. All three Gospels include the startling statement to the paralytic, "your sins are forgiven" (Luke 5:20). This text alone would be sufficient ground for questioning the view that the model of baptism in the Gospels involved cleansing by the water of baptism. Rather, the impression is given that the helpless man is first forgiven by Jesus, and this leads to his healing. All three Gospels go on to state that the healing of the paralytic is evidence that the Son of Man has "authority on earth to forgive sins." The words "on earth" could be a claim that Jesus' word of forgiveness on earth effects forgiveness in heaven. This would rightly be viewed as blasphemy by any Jewish theologian. How much more would the use of baptism with water to effect forgiveness be viewed as blasphemous? All three Gospels are clear that what is being done is the forgiving of sins *on earth,* and Luke has already explained in the Song of Zechariah that it is this community of forgiveness on earth that gives knowledge of God's salvation (Luke 1:77).

In view of the many references to the assurance of forgiveness in the Psalms it would be difficult to conceive of the early church believing that forgiveness, in that sense, could only be imparted by Christian baptism. On the other hand, the logic of our discipleship model is very powerful at this point. Of course *God* was able to forgive sins in the Old Testament. What is new is that large numbers of ordinary people, branded as sinners and outcasts by the Pharisaic system, suddenly found themselves accepted for table fellowship by the great prophet and Messiah, Jesus himself. He told them they were forgiven, and the churches were later to continue what "Jesus began to do and teach" (Acts 1:1). The Good News was, therefore, that all kinds of sinners, later including Samaritans, Roman soldiers, barbarians, and the like, could be assured of their sins being forgiven and washed away in baptism by the community that took them in. This experience would, in turn, help them grasp the salvation and forgiveness of God. But it would indeed be blasphemy to imagine that all the baptized were automatically washed and given places in heaven in an eternal sense. The function of baptism in the discipleship model is to make learners, and the Good News is that no one is too sinful or too far away from God's people to be cleansed and accepted. "What God has cleansed, you must not call common" (Acts 10:15).

Our interpretation is confirmed by the next passage, also found in all three synoptic Gospels, where Jesus sits at table with Levi and his company of disreputable cronies (Luke 5:29-32). The sequence is important. First the sinners are invited and welcomed. Then Jesus eats with them, and finally the suggestion is made that in the company of the forgiven their healing can take place. "Those who are well have no need of a physician, but those who are sick; I have not come to call the righteous, but sinners to repentance." Presumably this story was retold often in the early churches as an explanation and justification for the extraordinary practices of welcoming all and sundry to baptism, eating together in the communion feast, and trusting that this mixed multitude would be changed and healed by the work of the Holy Spirit.

Luke alone records Jesus' words to the Pharisee at dinner concerning the woman "who was a sinner" (Luke 7:36-50). Not only does Jesus accept the woman, permitting her to touch him at table by anointing him, but he explains that having been forgiven much she loves the more. Admittedly, verse 47 may be translated to suggest that much loving results in sins being forgiven, but the whole logic of the section is that the woman is first accepted as forgiven in Jesus' company, and that is why she loves. We should therefore translate the Greek conjunction *hoti* in its consecutive sense, "her many sins are forgiven [by me] with the result that she loves much" rather than, as in the RSV, "her sins, which are many, are forgiven, for she loved much." The latter makes no sense in the context of Jesus' parable (verses 40-43), which would belong to a model suggesting that not baptism, but much loving, effects forgiveness.

The three parables in Luke 15 (the lost sheep, the lost coin, the lost son) are introduced with the Pharisees and scribes objecting to tax collectors and sinners all drawing near to Jesus: "this man receives sinners and eats with them." Jesus' reception of sinners and his eating with them is what the parables illustrate, and these parables would have been used by the Christians in the New Testament Church to justify and explain the church's practice of baptism. We certainly cannot see how the parable of the Prodigal Son could relate to the cleansing model of baptism; the removal of original sin in heaven is not in view. The joy in heaven is over a sinner who repents, and repentance is not pictured as overwhelming contrition for sin, but rather as a sinner turning to accept forgiveness on earth. This parable fits the Discipleship model of baptism perfectly. The wayward son is forgiven unconditionally, immediately accepted into the family, with the end in view of beginning to learn the new lifestyle that is required in the family. As we have already noted, there is not one parable in Luke's gospel that would suggest the need of baptism to effect the cleansing of sin in an eternal sense.

## Baptism and the Holy Spirit
Our model also helps us to see why baptism is described as imparting both the forgiveness of sins and the Holy Spirit, and why these two gifts should be so closely linked: "Be baptized every one of you in the name of Jesus Christ for the forgiveness of your sins; and you shall receive the gift of the Holy Spirit" (Acts 2:38). Since we are baptized into a school of the Holy Spirit, all that the Holy Spirit is able to give in and through that school is given in baptism.[8] The Holy Spirit is to animate, supervise, bring freedom, and encourage prayer, love, and worship. Admittedly churches may be taken over by false prophets, fall into legalism, or quench the Spirit, but that is not in view when a Spirit-filled church adds disciples to its number.

Nor should we suggest that the Holy Spirit is unable to do his work outside the circle of the baptized. In the second verse of the Bible we find the Holy Spirit already moving

over the waters in creation (Gen. 1:2), and he worked
powerfully among many leaders and prophets of the Old
Testament. All that we need to remember in connection
with baptism is that the Holy Spirit was appointed to continue the discipling and teaching work of Jesus, and he
does it mainly through the various gifts of the Spirit in
churches which are schools of the Holy Spirit. Since baptism was the normal method of enrollment in such schools,
it is therefore appropriate to view baptism as instrumental in imparting the Spirit. On the other hand, if a
person is baptized, but, for any reason, is not taught by
the Holy Spirit, we need not posit an invisible presence of
the Spirit in his heart.

**The Spirit Given Before Baptism**
There are the special cases where the Holy Spirit was
already given before baptism. When Peter was invited to
Caesarea by the centurion Cornelius he found a group of
devout but unbaptized Gentiles. At that time it had been
unthinkable for total foreigners to be baptized into the
growing schools of the Holy Spirit. Having already been
warned by a vision not to call foreigners unclean, Peter
observes the evident outpouring of the Holy Spirit among
them, and hastens to register them by baptism (Acts
10:1-48). The logic is inescapable: "Can any one forbid
water for baptizing these people who have received the
Holy Spirit just as we have?" (Acts 10:47). Every school
registrar can think of cases where students were already
in class and doing assignments before the registration
process caught up with them.

Some missionaries have operated on a church model
which requires evidence of the Holy Spirit's work in the
heart of believers before baptism. Evidently our loving
God will not penalize the converts for that. But, as we
will see in our final chapter on Mission, such a procedure
will almost certainly slow down church growth. According

to this Probationary model, converts were already being taught in the church, for a longer or shorter period before baptism. But we have shown that such catechumens do not appear anywhere in the New Testament. Nobody was asked to show evidence of the power of the Holy Spirit in his life before being registered by baptism.

### The Samaritans Receive the Spirit After a Delay

Our model also throws light on the converse process, as it occurred in Samaria. Theologians of all schools have equivocated about the curious fact that the Samaritan converts were baptized by Philip, but apparently did not receive the Holy Spirit. It was not until the apostles at Jerusalem heard of this unusual situation, and came down and prayed, with the laying on of hands, that the Spirit was given.

Consider a marvellous new kind of school with brilliant and loving teachers, whose revolutionary methods have transformed children who were previously dull and unteachable. The time comes to open other schools so that a greater number of pupils can benefit. A field man visits a neighboring town, tells of the school and its achievements, and finds tremendous interest. He enrolls a group of new candidates and sends a message back saying that all is now ready for another school to start. A group of teachers from the parent school comes down two days later, and as the children are gathered, teaching begins, and the results begin to show immediately. In the educational world there are many such cases of enrollment a few days before classes begin. Missionaries, too, will frequently describe an enthusiastic response and the call from a neighboring area for a church to be organized. In such cases the book of Acts suggests that the baptisms can be immediate, and help can then be called in to inaugurate the new church with prayer for the Holy Spirit to begin his work.

If we say that the teaching of the Holy Spirit only begins after admission into the school of the Holy Spirit, do we then deny the work of the Holy Spirit in bringing people into the school? In the case of Philip are we to say that when multitudes heard his preaching, unclean spirits were cast out, the sick were healed, and there was much joy, none of this was the work of the Holy Spirit? Evidently not. The gift of being an evangelist is a gift of the Holy Spirit. The evangelist, by the power of the Spirit, was to gain a hearing for the Good News, and proclaim that the Messiah was risen from the dead. The church was to take in and teach those who wanted God's salvation. All who wished to enter the school were baptized, and teaching began immediately, or as soon as apostles could come and organize a new school.

We can assume that many who enthusiastically entered the growing churches did so after hearing a preliminary proclamation by an evangelist. Some of these would have been impressed by miracles of exorcism and healing. Others might have wanted to ask questions before baptism. None of these preliminaries were, however, made conditions for baptism. There is no example of an apostle asking "Have you really understood who Jesus was?", or "Are you sure that he can heal and cast out devils?", or "Do you feel that the Holy Spirit is convincing you that you should join this school?" We have already seen the pointlessness of checking up on behavior or good intentions. The fact of coming for baptism was evidence enough.

I do not want to get involved in the difficult theological problems raised by the charismatic movement. I might venture the observation that most of the best results of the movement have been in the rediscovery of the church as a community in which the Holy Spirit does his work in a rich variety of ways. If we picture a local church as a school of the Holy Spirit we should expect a variety of different gifts to be evident. In many cases a new disciple introduced into such a fellowship would show signs of being changed by the Holy Spirit from the first day. It is a fact that a previously frustrated child entering the class of a really good teacher, often changes dramatically within a few hours. How much more so in the school supervised by the Holy Spirit himself?

As soon as we begin thinking in New Testament terms, we are conscious that many of our present churches hardly permit the Holy Spirit to begin his work. That is not an argument for changing the practice of baptism. It is an argument for changing what happens *after* baptism.

### Baptism as Sacrament
The old Church of England catechism told us that a sacrament was an outward and visible sign of an inward and spiritual grace. If baptism is the outward and visible sign of registration in the school of Christ, what then is the corresponding inward and spiritual grace? If our model is correct, the grace is not some private, invisible influence on the heart. The grace is the sum of all that the Holy Spirit intends to do in the hearts and lives of the baptized, and if churches were schools where the Holy Spirit did his work, the grace would begin to be exercised with baptism. It is to be hoped that that is what many churches are now recovering in many exciting movements of renewal.

### Regeneration and Faith
At the end of the last chapter I distinguished three kinds of faith in relation to baptism:

*1 Faith to enroll* by baptism, as in the book of Acts.

*2 Faith as a movement towards the light,* as in John 3:18-21 and Heb. 10:39-11:16.

*3 Justification by faith,* as a doctrine to be understood. In the interpretation I have suggested for the new birth in this chapter it is the first kind of faith that relates to the new birth. Thus "to all who received him, who believed in his name, he gave power to become children of God; who were born, not of blood nor of the will of man, but of God" (John 1:12, 13). In crossing the Red Sea, those who decided to cross with their families were regenerate in that sense. The question of heart direction is quite different. As I argued in the last chapter, children, retarded persons, the untaught, and many who lived before Christ, may have had hearts which were right with God but who could not have accepted Jesus Christ in any intellectual way.

## Questions for Study and Discussion

1   Reread the story of Nicodemus in John 3, and ask yourself what it meant for this great rabbi to be born again.
2   How does the new birth in the Discipleship model of the church differ from what is taught about the new birth among other Christians that you know?
3   "The Discipleship model of baptism is clearly instrumental." What does the author say is actually effected in baptism? How does Christian baptism compare with the baptism of the Jews into Moses in the Red Sea (1 Cor. 10:1-12)?
4   The church is the circle of those who are learning to accept and give God's forgiveness. Discuss whether this is true in your own church.
5   When did you first experience the church as a community in which the Holy Spirit does his work in a rich variety of ways?

## Prayer

*"Jesus, I thank you for saying to so many and to me 'your sins are forgiven.' I long to experience the Holy Spirit teaching me, guiding me, producing his fruit, developing my gift, helping me to pray and worship. Free your church to be an accepting, Spirit-filled community."*

## Footnotes

[1] The questionable addition of the condition for baptism "if you believe with all your heart," in Acts 8:37, is evidence that baptismal rigor began soon after the apostolic period. By the time of Hippolytus (c. AD 170-236) an elaborate system of probation for catechumens had been invented, as expressed in the *Apostolic Tradition* [Latin edition by E. Hauler, Leipzig, 1900], Gregory Dix, ed., (London: SPCK, 1937).

[2] G. R. Beasley-Murray, *Baptism in the New Testament,* London: Macmillan & Co., (New York: St. Martin's Press, 1962), pp. 263-264. See also David Pawson's admission that the language of baptism is strongly instrumental, and the rite is "efficacious," "actually effecting what it signifies." David Pawson and Colin Buchanan, *Infant Baptism Under Cross-Examination,* (Bramcote, Notts.: Grove Books, 1974), p. 14.

[3] Proponents of believers' baptism would of course agree that some things are effected in baptism, such as a public witness to one's faith. Their point is that the spiritual experience of faith in Christ and the assurance of forgiveness, which together are viewed as the new birth, must precede baptism. On their view baptism does not effect the new birth.

[4] Many evangelical Anglicans would agree with Baptists that baptism does not effect the new birth, but would still claim that it is effective in eliciting faith.

[5] Anglican *Book of Common Prayer* communion service. p. 334.

[6] Very few post-Vatican-II, Roman Catholic theologians would accept the Cleansing model of baptism set out in the Introduction. That model implies that none of the unbaptized will be in heaven.

[7] C. S. Lewis, *The Great Divorce,* New York: Macmillan, 1946.

[8] In an important article, Dr. B. E. Thiering argues that at Qumran, purification by the Spirit of holiness was not effected by the water but rather associated with entry into the community. She therefore posits another rite, after water baptism, to effect the real initiation. Using our Discipleship model, a simple solution emerges: that water baptism adds members to the community and purification is effected by being in the community where the Spirit does his work. B. E. Thiering, "Inner and Outer Cleansing at Qumran as a Background to New Testament Baptism", *New Testament Studies,* 26 (1980), No. 2, pp. 266-277.

# Fellowship

*So those who received his word*
*were baptized, and there were added*
*that day about three thousand*
*souls. And they devoted*
*themselves to the apostles'*
*teaching and fellowship*
*(Acts 2:41, 42).*

# 7

WE HAVE SEEN THAT BAPTISM, as practiced in the New Testament, was the means appointed by Jesus for enrolling learners in the school of the Holy Spirit. We noted that for most of us the word "school" has a somewhat negative connotation. If the Christian Church were merely an educational agency it would be unattractive indeed.

But add the word "fellowship" and the whole picture changes and brightens. The crusty Victorian schoolteacher drilling Latin verbs into his pupils made no allowance for fellowship. He wanted none between himself and his pupils, and as little as possible among the children themselves. He was intent on academic training, and fellowship was seen as a distraction. But what does *Christian fellowship* mean? Some people think of social gatherings, serving tea and pot luck suppers. Others look back nostalgically to fervent groups singing together the old-time hymns. For many men, the only happy memories of church come from being part of a work team pouring concrete for a new floor or fixing up a summer camp. In each of these activities there is obviously an ingredient of fellowship, but not necessarily of Christian *koinonia*. This New Testament Greek term for fellowship has a distinctive quality to it. It may involve social gatherings, singing, and practical work, but it exists apart from them. It infuses and transforms all typically Christian activities.

Here is a working definition of *koinonia:* "A group of people who accept each other as sinners with a view to being changed by God." Christian fellowship involves accepting and being accepted in a group of sinners. We make no claim to be good people. Many of those who never darken the doors of our churches are far more noble, upright, and loving than we are. We do not pretend to have attained any standard of spirituality or saintliness, like the Pharisees. We are all sinners.

And of course "sinners" does not just mean the gross sins like murder, drunkenness, immorality, and bank robbery. We define sin in terms of our end product. When God has finished with us we have to be absolutely perfect.[1] I admit that if you are to enjoy me forever in heaven I need a huge amount of changing! The least imperfection in the light of heaven would be unbearable. Sin is therefore anything and everything that will need to change, in me, before I am fit to be your fellow in the eternal City of God.

### There Is a Doctor in the House!

Now Jesus claimed to be the doctor for sin. He undertook to heal and perfect sinners. When the Pharisees objected that his friends were those who made no pretense to being righteous, he answered "Those who are well have no need of a physician, but those who are sick; I came not to call the righteous, but sinners" (Mark 2:17). That means that

Christian churches are not only schools but hospitals, and hospitals are for the sick. All Christians are patients expecting to be made perfectly whole by Jesus Christ. Because I am a Christian you should assume that I am in need of healing. And I assume that you also as a fellow Christian have a great deal of sin sickness that Jesus is dealing with. That is the basis of our relationship in the church.

Jesus made this very clear in the parable of the unforgiving servant. Having been forgiven ten thousand talents' (or several million dollars') worth of misappropriation he goes out and grabs by the throat a fellow servant who owes him twenty dollars. Peter was irritated at the necessity of forgiving a friend seven times, but Jesus said "not seven times but seventy times seven" (Matt. 18:21-35). So when I meet you as a Christian I must expect to forgive you many faults. You will also find many faults to forgive in me. Much will need to change for me to be your fellow in heaven. Some of our sins may be common to both of us. Others will seem strange and incomprehensible to you: "How on earth can he be so selfish, unfeeling, fussy . . . ?" As I observe you and you observe me more closely we must learn not to be shocked at each other's behavior.

**Faith to Expect Change**
But of course that degree of acceptance does not alone constitute Christian fellowship. The drunks on skid row accept each other too. Many groups of friends have an amazing tolerance of each other's sins. Our definition specifies those "who accept each other as sinners with a view to being changed by God." This means that you look at me as I am, with a fair knowledge of my faults, and then you must picture me as perfected. You must imagine me cleansed of all that displeases you, a fellow citizen in the City of God. That introduces a huge measure of faith into

Christian fellowship. The drunks on skid row accept each other, but they expect no change for the better. For them, things can only get worse until death ends the increasing stupor.

## Leave it to God

Now, we come to the third part of Christian fellowship and the most difficult to enact. I accept you as a sinner with a number of faults. I picture you as perfected when God has finished his work in you. But then I am tempted to undertake the process of change myself. When I notice you are addicted to drugs, easily depressed, shy, touchy, and very angry both with yourself and with any who try to get too close to you, I decide that the obvious first thing to correct is your lack of self-control. I begin by kidding you, nagging you, then lecturing you and trying to shame you. I may conscript others to join me in applying moral pressure. In some cases we may succeed. Some churches have developed very effective methods for changing sinners. But that is not part of our definition of fellowship. "To be changed by God" means that we leave it to God to do the changing in his own way and according to his perfect sequence.

God may not decide to begin with your addiction. Perhaps, as he discerns the thoughts and intents of your heart, he sees that you use drugs because of loneliness or frustration. And you are frustrated because you find it hard to relate to people. In your case that is because you have never known what love is. You cannot picture God as a loving Father because your own father treated you so abominably. These are some of the knotted tangles of causality that pyschiatrists try to disentangle, and Christians should recognize their work as a necessary part of the healing arts. The difficulty is that psychiatrists are often unable to do the unraveling, and even when they succeed there is still much more to be corrected, from God's point of view. Together with whatever help friends, and family, and modern medicine are able to give, my acceptance of you must include a steady faith that God is in control and he will work in and through all his diverse means to complete your perfection.

### Praying Without Interfering
This trust in God to change you is not a passive thing. Prayer is a deliberate handing-over of one's fellow to be changed by God himself. That is the most loving thing I can do for you, and the greatest ground of fellowship. It is at once incredibly easy, so that a child can do it, and supremely difficult, because we find every reason for either ignoring or interfering in the lives of others. *Prayer neither ignores nor interferes.* It is the genuine loving support that every Christian needs. If I speak out of turn I will do more harm than good. I will get the sequence of change wrong. But if I pray and watch God doing his loving work in you, I can be interested without interfering, loving without selfish possessiveness.

God the Father, God the Son, and God the Holy Spirit can be trusted to work all things together for your good. That means that every event and circumstance of your life, whether apparently good or apparently bad, is a sign of God's loving activity. "The Lord disciplines him whom he loves ... for what son is there whom his father does not discipline?" (Heb. 12:6-7). So I watch God the Father dealing with you as a son or daughter. I also watch Jesus Christ come alongside you, as a friend, as a brother, as an example, as your captain, as your king, as your companion in battle. And simultaneously I see the Holy Spirit showing you things I could never point out, teaching spiritual truths in a way I could never explain, helping you to pray according to the mind of God, producing one, then another of his beautiful fruits. As all this happens I rejoice and give thanks. And you are doing the same for me. So we have fellowship.

## Unity in Diversity

Watching the Holy Spirit change you will also have its
perplexities. If, as Paul teaches, the Church is a body,
then the Holy Spirit will produce many different kinds of
Christians, all as different from each other as bone is from
liver, teeth from brain tissue. As I begin to pray for you
I don't know what you are going to become. And some
changes will be very hard to understand. You too may find
my pattern of gifts strangely different from yours. And
yet we are to have fellowship. That is why Paul stresses
the need to keep the unity of our fellowship at the same
time as encouraging our differences. "With all lowliness
and meekness, with patience, forbearing one another in
love, eager to maintain the unity of the Spirit in the bond
of peace. There is one body and one Spirit" (Eph. 4:2-4).

## Change by Creating Guilt

The main difficulty about real Christian fellowship is that
many in our churches are afraid that mutual acceptance
would interfere with the recognition of sin. They feel that
without public rebuke and remorse on the part of erring
church members there will be no progress in holiness.
Imagine a ski school where every time somebody crashes
on the hill and breaks a ski all the other skiers gather
around the unfortunate victim. As they point their finger
they chant "You have fallen. Leave our ski slope." The
only way back into favor is by falling on one's knees,
admitting one's awful failure, and earnestly promising
never to fall again.

But how long would such a ski school stay open? And
even if it did stay in business, would it produce better
skiers? Actually the fear of falling and of being humiliated
is the biggest hindrance to real learning progress. And
yet many churches try to operate on such a dismal puni-
tive system. No wonder Christians are paralyzed. No
wonder outsiders shun us like the plague. We all need

the assurance of total acceptance to make progress in the direction of the perfection promised by Jesus Christ.

## The Place of Discipline
What then should we do about discipline? If we baptize individuals and families without probation, undertaking to love them when they are still horribly deficient in Christian perfection, how can our churches survive? Taking in all comers would fill our churches with the same kind of mixed multitude that came out of Egypt in the first Exodus. But isn't this exactly what Jesus seemed to recommend by his own friendship with sinners? And did he not tell us to compel people to come in to the banquet from the highways and hedges, specifying "both good and bad" (Luke 14:21-23, Matt. 22:9, 10)?

## Apostasy
We therefore need to disentangle the various aspects of church discipline which made the early churches' open admission policy workable. First we must face the fact of apostasy, which apparently occurred among a large number of the disciples of Jesus (John 6:60, 66). Warnings about the dangers of falling away from the faith occur throughout the Epistle to the Hebrews. Apostasy is closely linked with unbelief. "Take care, brethren, lest there be in any of you an evil, unbelieving heart, leading you to fall away from the living God" (Heb. 3:12). Here the Greek verb is *apostenai,* which means to go away, withdraw, fall away, become apostate.[2] Then the writer stresses the need for Christians to exhort one another "that none of you may be hardened by the deceitfulness of sin. For we share in Christ, if only we hold our first confidence firm to the end" (Heb. 3:12, 13). Here a comparison is made with what happened in the Exodus from Egypt. Those who failed to go on into Canaan are described as "disobedient"; they were unable to enter the promised land "because of

unbelief" (Heb. 3:15-19). In this case they did not physically separate themselves from God's people, but they were still apostate in their hearts. The application of this condition to the people of the New Exodus suggests that disobedience or unbelief (the Greek root *apeitheo* is the same) is a sin of the baptized. Later in the Epistle the writer uses the word "faith" as the opposite to shrinking back. He is glad that his readers are among "those who have faith and keep their souls" (Heb. 10:35-39).

In chapter 5 I argued that faith is an attitude, a direction, a walk like Abraham's faith. Those who teach that we are justified by a decision of faith, followed by baptism, have great difficulties with the apostasy passages in the Epistle to the Hebrews. It is quite clear that the ones to whom these warnings are addressed are baptized Christians, who have already learned and benefited from the work of the Holy Spirit in a Christian church. "It is impossible to restore again to repentance those who have once been enlightened, who have tasted the heavenly gift, and have become partakers of the Holy Spirit, and have tasted the goodness of the word of God and the powers of the age to come, if they then commit apostasy ..." (Heb. 6:4-6).[3]

What then is this apostasy among the baptized? It is not that the faithful are sinless and by contrast, apostates are particularly wicked. Paul admitted to a great deal of sin and failure both in himself and in his churches. *Apostasy is a refusal to accept further change by the Holy Spirit.* Perhaps our image of the school can again help our understanding. What makes it impossible for a pupil to benefit further from a school? It is not dullness, or naughtiness, or failure to complete the assignments. It is a stubborn rejection of contact with the school, an unwillingness to believe in the teachers, a refusal to be influenced by them, so that growth and learning ceases. In the Christian church the equivalent apostasy from Jesus Christ is a rejection of the teaching and transforming work of the Holy Spirit. It is not necessary to make a formal denial of the faith, or to engage in any particularly heinous crime, or even to withdraw physically from a church. All that is required for apostasy is to shrink back from the continuing influence of the Holy Spirit in our lives.

Since the opposite of justification by faith is insistence on being justified by one's own goodness, such apostasy will be expressed in self-righteousness. This is why Paul was so upset by what happened among the Galatians. They had evidently been baptized into Christ, and had experienced the consequent teaching and transforming power of the Holy Spirit in the school. Under the influence of false teaching they had begun turning back to works of the law for their justification. In effect, they were withdrawing from the Holy Spirit. "You are severed from Christ, you who would be justified by the law; you have fallen from grace." Paul then contrasts the true Christian faith attitude: "through the Spirit, by faith, we wait for the hope of righteousness" (Gal. 5:4, 5). It is as if a branch, which has been grafted in and begun living by the sap of the vine, now closes itself off from further influence of the tree. Separated from contact with the tree, and depending on its own goodness alone, it is dead and lost.

**False Teachers, Inquisition and Exclusion**
The second area for discipline, or discipling, or training (the ideas are all connected) is the problem of false teachers, prophets, and apostles. It seems that these abounded in the New Testament churches. Some false teachers can be corrected by the gentle explanation or exhortation of a church leader (2 Tim. 2:24-26; Jude 17-23). Others have already rejected the teaching of the Holy Spirit, but they may decide to remain in the churches for their own advantage (Acts 20:29-30; 1 Tim. 4:1-3; 6:3-5; 2 Pet. 2:1-3). It is these who must be tested and

exposed for what they are, in which case they will probably leave (1 John 2:18, 19; 4:1-6; 2 John 9-11). When false
teachers are strongly established, it may be impossible to
silence them, in which case it is better to avoid them
(2 Tim. 3:1-9; Titus 1:9-13). In view of the fact that good
and bad fruits take time to ripen, we can imagine that
there was much difficult heart searching before decisions
could be made.

We should distinguish the strong measures prescribed
for false teachers from the gentle discipline for disciples.
It is striking that Jesus' fierce words are directed at the
religious teachers of his day. They laid impossible religious burdens on ordinary people (Matt. 23:1-36). He does
not have one word of exclusion for drunks, prostitutes,
and members of the local tax-collecting mafia.

There is only one case of exclusion for gross sin in the
New Testament. A man is having a sexual relationship
with his step-mother, while his father is presumably still
alive. He apparently insists on flaunting his immorality
in the assembly of Christians, and they seem to be indifferent to what is happening (1 Cor. 5:1-13). Even in this
extreme case Paul is very concerned in his next letter to
have the disciplined brother restored and loved in case he
is "overwhelmed with excessive sorrow" (2 Cor. 2:6-8).
What would be an equivalent in our modern situation?

Again let us test our school analogy. How bad does a
student have to be to be expelled from a high school class?
A good teacher may know that a student is using and
selling hard drugs, but will keep teaching him in the hope
that he will make it through school and come to his senses.
But what if the boy comes to class, lights up a joint, and
blatantly begins to sell drugs while the class is going on?
Obviously at that point discipline must be exercised, and
the student sent to the principal. Exclusion is only required if the flagrant behavior of one makes the work of
the whole class impossible.

Similarly with a local church, the objective is that Christians should be able to grow in the Spirit. There is no point in having an inquisition to discover every case of private sin. And how many of us would be left in church if we were removed for envy, pride, harshness, gluttony, not loving God or our neighbor or our spouses, or gossip? On the other hand, we can think of cases where the teaching process becomes impossible. Paul mentions drunkenness at the communion table (1 Cor. 11:21, 22). One Anglican church had to exclude from discussion groups three fellows who insisted on hogging the floor with bizarre teaching. We might have to restrict the activities of someone who came in to rob the offering plate or disturb the worship. Though we can agree that the state has no business in the bedrooms of the nation, we might have to call the police to eject those involved in sexual immorality performed on church premises.

### Acceptable and Unacceptable Sins?
Our difficulty is that churches have tacitly suggested that pride, avarice, hatred, false witness, lack of love, and worry are sins acceptable among the church membership, but we must express righteous indignation and throw out the sexual sins. Consider for example the problem of homosexuality. As we use the Discipleship model of church discipline we do not have to answer thorny questions as to whether homosexuality is deviance from the norm, or a sickness to be cured, or a particularly heinous sin that must be cut out like cancer. A homosexual obviously has a different pattern of sins from, say, a macho type heterosexual, or an insensitive extrovert, or a "don't-touch-me" prude, or a chronic hypochondriac, or a hard-driving workaholic. Whatever our pattern of sins, Jesus Christ invites us to be baptized, to take Communion, to look to the Holy Spirit, to be open to being changed by him in due course. It is unreasonable to require proof of change before

the Holy Spirit has had time to penetrate our inner being, surround us with love, fill us with new fruits and gifts.

What is not acceptable is for behavior which is a clear denial of Christian love to be propagated as the norm in our Christian education program. Though we are all tainted with prejudice, we cannot permit racial or class hatred to be taught from our pulpits. Worry about money, miserly greed, and stinginess are sins which may be corrected by the Holy Spirit in our churches, but we cannot let mammon worship replace Holy Communion. Similarly there comes a point at which we will have to muzzle or restrict an individual or a group attempting to take over a church in order to propagate homosexual behavior which is an obvious denial of Christian love. At what point that line has to be drawn will involve much heart searching. What if a Bible study group becomes an occasion for group sex? What if a member is having sex with the choir boys or the girls' craft club? What do we do with the pimp who recruits in the church for his trade? Or the leader of the young people's group who recommends a gay lifestyle? The question we have to ask is "Does this behavior, or this teaching, or this permissiveness interfere with the whole church's growth in love and joy and the Holy Spirit?" If it does, we at least have to be concerned, we have to pray, we may need to talk to an individual. There may come a point at which disciplinary exclusion from the group is required, but let no one assume that such action is easy.

I suggest that the one case of exclusion for a sexual sin was of this nature. The fellow in Corinth not only slept with his step-mother, but insisted on publicizing it and soliciting the approval of the Corinthian church, probably to the extent of coming hand-in-hand with the woman in question to take Communion. Whether or not this was the case, I suggest that exclusion for a time was necessary to preserve the Christian education process from total confusion.

One other passage of Scripture is usually cited as an argument for excommunication for moral transgressions. Jesus mentions the problem of a brother who has sinned against you. First go and see him alone, then take one or two others along, and finally bring the case before the church. If there is still refusal to listen, the person should then be viewed as an outsider (Matt. 18:15-17). Some churches have made this into a procedure for checking the sins of others, and bringing moral pressure to bear on the unfortunate victims. It would seem much more natural to view this procedure as comparable to the method suggested by Paul for dealing with lawsuits between Christians. "When one of you has a grievance against a brother, does he dare go to law before the unrighteous instead of the saints?" (1 Cor. 6:1-5). In that case we are not looking for a method of excommunicating offending brothers but of righting a wrong done. If a Christian has defrauded us we are to try and get the matter settled among Christians first. Finally, if the offender has refused a settlement among the brethren, we consider him an outsider, taking him to court if necessary. Paul, however, hopes that litigation among Christians will not be necessary at all.

If Jesus' teaching in Matthew 18 is similar to Paul's instructions in 1 Corinthians 6 and relates to legal differences among Christians, how can we apply it to hounding other church members when we discover their sin? As we have already seen, we are all sinners in various ways, and fellowship means accepting each other as sinners with a view to being changed by God.

### Discipling—Who Does It?
This changing by God then brings us to the most important aspect of discipline in the New Testament. It is not other Christians who are appointed to correct our moral failures, but God himself. After quoting the passage about

God's discipline from Proverbs, the Epistle to the Hebrews tells us that God disciplines his children. A sure sign that we are loved by God, and viewed as his children, is the fact that we are disciplined. "What son is there whom his father does not discipline?" (Heb. 12:5-11). Where unbelievers curse their luck and learn nothing from the chastisements of life, Christians should become sensitive to the firm hand of God in their lives.

The most awesome case of God's disciplinary judgment in a church was the sudden death of Ananias, and then of his wife, when they agreed to lie deliberately to the congregation, and therefore to the Holy Spirit (Acts 5:1-11). Paul explains in another connection that all those who share in the bread and wine of the communion service are subject to God's own chastening. Similarly, any child adopted into a loving family will find that firm discipline is part of the new parents' love. The ideal is to learn by taking proper care to do what we are expected to do. But if we are careless, God as a loving Father can be relied on to apply his chastisement (1 Cor. 11:27-33). We note that it is God who does the disciplining, not the church authorities. Nor should we assume that God's physical discipline on earth entails hell in the hereafter.

In this connection I would like to suggest (without being able to prove my case) that excommunication from the bread and the wine of Holy Communion was never used as a disciplinary method in the New Testament. It would be comparable to permanently refusing a child a place at the family dinner table. A child may be rebuked for misbehavior. He may be sent away from a meal for stubborn insolence or lying. But excommunication from the family table is not compatible with treating a child as a member of the family. And to use rejection from the family as a threat to bring a child into line is a form of the most sordid barbarity. Such barbarity has recurred in the history of many churches, but it is time we recognized the perversity of the practice for what it is. I suggest that the idea of ex-communication came into the churches as a legalistic approach to church discipline based on a total misconception of God's love and grace. It would be very hard to find any case in church history where it has, in the long run, promoted genuine spirituality as opposed to Pharisaism.

### The Case for Excommunication: "No Case"

I have admitted that I cannot prove my case. On the other hand the weakness of the case for excommunication should be noted. How would we prove that ecclesiastical excommunication was prescribed in the New Testament? The only text that is remotely relevant is: "I wrote to you not to associate with anyone who bears the name of brother if he is named (the RSV translation "is guilty of" is a mistranslation) an immoral man, or greedy, or an idolater, or a drunkard, or a robber—not even to eat with such a one" (1 Cor. 5:11, RSV corrected). The first thing to note is that there is no procedure laid down for a judicial hearing by the elders. The natural translation is that each Christian must decide who is to be excluded from his fellowship. The expression "is named" suggests that there is a distinction between a sinner who has failed and the person who views the sin with self-complacent pride, and has built a reputation for sinning, with no intention of changing his ways. The member of the church who blatantly declares that he organizes drinking parties with the object of getting drunk or feels that the buying of sex for money is commendatory, or recommends idolatry in the church, or recruits for the local mafia—such a person is rejecting what the Christian church stands for. When such people are in power in a church it is, in any case, impossible to excommunicate them. What can be done is for Christians to talk to them on a person-to-person basis, and then refuse to associate with them if they persist in such an attitude.

There is not one reference to excommunication from the bread and wine in the seven letters of the book of Revelation. Who would make such a decision, and how would the case be heard and tried? The Epistle of Jude refers to "blemishes on your love feasts" and tells us explicitly that there were licentious persons, deniers of Jesus Christ, sexual perverts, and divisive people, in those churches. Surely there would have been some reference to excommunication here, if it had been deemed appropriate. Instead the appeal is strictly personal. "But you, beloved, build yourselves up... pray... keep yourselves in the love of God ... convince some, who doubt, save some, by snatching them out of the fire" (Jude 20-22). I suggest that it is the same personal confrontation, with the possible result of personal refusal of Christian fellowship, which is in view in the case of Corinth.

What then of Paul's strong words concerning the communion service? "Whoever, therefore, eats the bread or drinks the cup of the Lord in an unworthy manner will be guilty of profaning the body and blood of the Lord. Let a man examine himself, and so eat of the bread and drink of the cup" (1 Cor. 11:27-28). This is not a mandate for excommunication by a church court. It refers to individuals examining themselves. Paul specifies the danger of partaking "without discerning the body" (v. 29) and the context shows that this refers to divisions, factions, selfishness and drunkenness at the table, and despising others (vv. 17-22). Such attitudes are extremely dangerous to Christ's body, and they may result in physical sickness and even death (vv. 29-30). We have no difficulty in understanding the psychosomatic effects of hatred, jealousy, anger, fear, and anxiety in our own bodies. We may find it hard to grasp the effects on a local church as the body of Christ in the way that Paul did. But whatever Paul meant it did not involve an inquisition into the private lives of members to exclude them, by a judicial act, from Communion.

I might add that the Roman Catholic hierarchy, in opposition to the better sense of the majority of its members, has maintained an automatic excommunication for divorced persons who remarry. The moral credibility lost by annulling the marriages of some, and excluding hundreds of thousands of other Christians who have admittedly failed in a sinful situation, is notorious. In other churches, except for some rigorous sects, excommunication is extremely rare, usually in cases of proven immorality of one kind or another. The whole procedure for making the decision is filled with such inconsistencies that most churches allow the idea of excommunication to stay in the books, but keep cases under the rug until forced to act by well-meaning members. The net result is that the world and the press, when it can get hold of the sordid details, is convinced that Christians view sexual abberration as a certain cause for going to hell, but consider sins such as pride and lack of love unimportant.

### The Communion Table—Place of Healing
I have belabored the point of the inappropriateness of excommunication from partaking of the bread and the wine. The reason is that the model of churches as schools for sinful disciples requires the admission of all the baptized to Communion. When sin and failure have occurred, the first requirement for spiritual restoration is that the person should be encouraged to return for healing at the family table. There the Holy Spirit can create the necessary contrition and restoration.

### Love or Legalism
The real question at issue is whether God has designed a church family where it is possible to include sinners of every kind. If he has, then surely he must have a way, by the Holy Spirit, to deal with the most heinous sins. And

that work of the Holy Spirit is contrasted again and again
with legalism. God uses the words of Scripture, the ex-
hortations of preachers, the love and concern of Christian
brothers and sisters, and the inner conviction of the Holy
Spirit in and through the worship of his people. There is
also the chastening hand of God, who works all things
together for good to train and perfect us. But wherever
ecclesiastical authorities take a hand in doing what God
alone can do, the results are uniformly dismal.

### Children at the Table

At this point we note again the implications of this model
of the church for the admission of children to the communion table. We argued that local churches are schools
of the Holy Spirit, and the bread and the wine is the heart
of their worship. Since little children can never be too
young to begin learning, they should be able to share in
the worship long before they can understand it. Children
eat in a family before they learn what the family means
to them. In fact it is eating together that nourishes family
life. We are not thinking merely of proteins and calories,
but of table fellowship, belonging, talking, enjoying one
another. That is why local churches are constituted and
nourished by eating and drinking together, and by all that
goes on at that feast. And since little children are never
too young to be adopted and loved in such a family of the
Holy Spirit, how can we think of excluding them from the
family table?

But are not babies too small to sit up at table, eat adult
food, and hold their own cup? In some ways they are but
that does not exclude them from our table. It is vital that
from their earliest days they remember belonging at the
table with us. They should never have to prove themselves, pass tests, believe, or make some commitment.
They should feel themselves totally loved and accepted as
full members of the family of God. Later they will respond

with gratitude, commitment, willingness to suffer, and so on, but those are not conditions but rather the fruits of already belonging.

### Divine Intervention
Finally we must include God's own discipline of local churches as churches. Even after Paul's careful apostolic work, some of his churches fell into confusion. The congregation in Corinth was divided by bitter sectarianism. Several of the seven churches of Asia Minor were taken over by false prophets. A repeated refrain in John's revelation to them was what Jesus the Lord of the churches would do with them. A point comes at which a lampstand has to be removed (Rev. 2:5), which must mean the termination of church life in that place. Sometimes the Lord of the church will war against false teachers with the sword of his mouth (Rev. 2:16). He may also hand a church over to terrible tribulation (Rev. 2:22, 23). There may be a sudden visitation like a thief in the night (Rev. 3:3), or he may spew a lukewarm church out of his mouth (Rev. 3:15, 16).

At what point does such a dramatic act by the Lord of the churches occur? Presumably when a congregation will not, or can no longer, perform its function as a school of the Holy Spirit. If false teachers have taken over, or the members are indifferent to their discipling task, the Lord himself will intervene. But we note that the allowing of persecution, or natural disaster, or the complete termination of church life, are all acts of God. There is no place for wars of religion to correct the doctrine of other churches. The lordship of Christ over his churches goes together with his instructions for taking in any seekers for teaching.

### Summary
We conclude that our task is, first to persuade people of all tribes and nations to be baptized and begin learning with

us. Second, we must ensure that the Holy Spirit is free to
superintend and control every aspect of his gracious work
in our churches. This will involve recognizing and muzz-
ling, where possible, the false teachers. When things get
out of hand, as they will in a certain proportion of our
churches, we look to Jesus Christ himself to intervene,
and we pray accordingly. Those who find it hard to believe
that the Holy Spirit can do his work, and that Jesus Christ
can intervene to rule his churches, are the ones who will
inevitably look for more rigorous methods of doing God's
work for him. They will be tempted to exclude undesira-
bles from baptism, to make it difficult for the family to eat
together, to threaten some kinds of sinners with excommunication, and to go to war, or at least disapprove
of, those who do not agree with them. It is to be hoped that
all churches are moving in the direction of abandoning
such methods in favor of a greater reliance on the Holy
Spirit.

### Questions for Study and Discussion

1   The definition of *koinonia*, or Christian fellowship, has three parts.
    Compare the practice of your own church under the first: "a group
    of people who accept each other as sinners." Do strangers to the
    churches get the impression that "we do not claim to be good
    people"?
2   How does the author say a church differs from the drunks on skid
    row? What kind of change should you expect in the more tiresome
    members of your church?
3   Go over your own prayer for others, for your family, for church
    members, in the light of the concept that "prayer neither ignores
    nor interferes." What is meant by "sequence of change"?
4   Why would the chanting of "you have fallen" not produce good
    results in a ski school? How about in a family? in a church? What
    kind of behavior *would* require exclusion from a ski school?
5   If we compare Holy Communion to a family eating together at the
    table, when should children be included, excluded, restored?

### Prayer

*"Thank you, Father, for Christian fellowship. I rejoice in those who*

*accept me as I am, and yet expect me to become a beautiful person. Help our church to be like a family under your loving discipline."*

## Footnotes

[1] The words translated "you must be perfect" in the Sermon on the Mount may equally well be translated "you will be perfect" (*esesthe oun humeis teleioi,* Matt. 5:48). In the Discipleship model Jesus would thus be setting out what he intends to achieve in perfecting his disciples. The verse has been given several other interpretations depending on the church model adopted, since there is no way to know what the verse means from the Greek words themselves.

[2] See Arndt and Gingrich, *A Greek-English Lexicon,* (University of Chicago Press, 1957), p. 126.

[3] Commenting on 1 Cor. 10, Oscar Cullmann speaks of "falling away from" or losing "irretrievably" the grace of baptism, and quotes the apostasy texts in Hebrews by way of explanation. *Baptism in the New Testament,* (London: SCM Press, 1950), p. 47.

# Mission

*"Go out quickly to the streets and*
*lanes of the city, and bring in the*
*poor and maimed and blind and lame*
*. . . . Go out to the highways and*
*hedges, and compel people to come in,*
*that my house may be filled"*
*(Luke 14:21-23).*

# 8

NOW, LET'S BE PRACTICAL. If our model is what underlies and explains the New Testament approach to baptism, how do we apply it in a parish? For the sake of simplicity, I will use the terminology of an Anglican or American Episcopalian type of local church; this is what I have been familiar with in three different continents, Britain, India, and North America. It is my hope that those of other denominations will understand and translate these principles in terms of other types of church organization. For Lutherans, Methodists, the Canadian United Church, Roman Catholics, Greek Orthodox, and Presbyterians, the translation will be simple. Those who delay the baptism of children from Christian homes till puberty, or till they can make a profession of faith, will need to substitute dedication or some similar rite to mark the entrance of the child into Christian teaching.

We begin with the object in view: to take in and teach as many as possible. We seek to obey the command, "Go ... make disciples of all nations, baptizing them in the name of the Father and of the Son and of the Holy Spirit, teaching them to observe all that I have commanded you" (Matt. 28:19-20).

So we persuade our own congregation to form themselves into a school for learners—not an old fashioned structure with a teacher lecturing rows of passive pupils, but rather a happy place, more like an open school, with newcomers welcome, and everyone learning at a different stage on his or her own level. We begin with what Jesus taught in the Gospels: learning to talk to God as a loving Father, to love our enemies, to forgive, to understand the Bible, to develop gifts and talents, to care about our neighbors. We can then proceed to the teaching of the Epistles both for new Christians, and for the very advanced.

If an individual, or a whole family, wishes to begin learning, we baptize them as soon as possible with a minimum of fuss. If they have already been baptized in any other church, we help them to continue their discipleship with us. We ask nothing of them, except that they come and learn. Our responsibility is to provide the facilities and the teachers needed. If we can't do that for them we have no right to baptize: it would be like enrolling students in a school that does not exist!

The key to our model of the church is that baptism is the beginning of teaching by the Holy Spirit. The baptism itself therefore tells you nothing about the qualities or intentions of the person baptized. It makes clear that this person or household is now to be taught by the Holy Spirit in the fellowship of our church. Thus the whole responsibility is taken from the candidates and given to our congregation. It is our responsibility to accept all comers, and to ensure that they are taught as much as they are able to receive. And our acceptance of unsatisfactory sinners is not to be passive: "let them come if they really want." Rather we are to *go and bring them in*. And if that does not fill our church, we are to "compel" others to come in. If we make it clear to them that they come in to learn (rather than to profess goodness) we may find many more willing to find out about Jesus Christ than we anticipate.

## No One Too Young to Learn
Once this principle is established, then the baptism (or dedication) of children will follow inevitably. No one is too young to learn. We pray for our babies in their cribs, teach them the name of Jesus along with "Dada" and "Mama," read them bedside stories from the Bible, and take them to worship with us even before they are weaned. If they are part of the school of Christ, and baptism is the entrance to that school, it makes no sense to delay till they can prove they have understood its teaching.

This acceptance of children for enrollment in the school of the Holy Spirit brings us to a serious objection: "You have suggested a kind of indiscriminate baptism, and we may agree to that for adults who make some kind of commitment. If you confine yourself to the children of parents who can be expected to teach their children, the argument still holds. But it is impossible to practice the indiscriminate baptism of thousands of children whose parents have no interest in teaching them, who *cannot* teach them because they themselves know nothing of the Christian faith, and who make no attempt to worship with God's people."

## The Relaxed Old Rector
Let us put the situation at its worst. Here is an Anglican or Episcopal church with an average of a hundred people meeting faithfully for worship on Sunday mornings. In the afternoon, the custom has been for christening parties at which parents turn up to have their children "done."

Some of these have phoned ahead to check the time. Others appear unannounced. None have any connection with the worshipping church except that they live in the parish, though in some cases a relative or friend has suggested that this is the most convenient place, and the rector is a kind old fellow who greets everyone very nicely and asks no awkward questions. Each baptism is recorded impressively in the register, and the proud mother receives a baptism certificate for her white-robed baby. After the service the family gathering enjoys the christening party, photographs are taken, and everyone is very satisfied that "the right thing" has been done.

### The Rigorous New Rector
Now an enthusiastic new rector comes to the parish, announcing "If that is indiscriminate baptism, I will have no part of it." He insists on an interview with every family before he will baptize their children. First of all he refuses all who come from outside his parish boundary. Next he insists on a confirmation certificate from each parent, or at least regular attendance from one of them.[1] The first year or two he has to bend a bit, and make exceptions, but by the time parents come with a second child for baptism, having made no attempt to come to church since the last one, he refuses adamantly. He sets up an impressive training program of several weeks of instruction and worship, which both parents must attend before the baptism. He also expects three-months notice of a proposed baptism,[2] and makes doubly sure by insisting that godparents are serious, practicing Anglicans. Within two years the new rector has cut down his stream of baptisms to a trickle, and virtually all infant baptisms involve children of members of the congregation.

These, then, are the two practices which are set in opposition in the usual debate between those in favor, and those opposed to indiscriminate baptism.[3] If I were forced to choose either of these alternatives I suspect I would have to leave parish ministry. The trouble is that the biblical practice of immediate baptism has never even been proposed, let alone practiced, and that is one reason for this book.[4]

Admittedly in Great Britain, where the Anglican Church of England and the Presbyterian Church of Scotland are state churches, the huge numbers wanting christening for their babies is viewed as a lamentable problem. In other parts of the world it would be viewed as a teaching opportunity. Our job is not to reduce the numbers to what we think we can manage, but to take seriously our job as teachers of the nations. That, then, gives us a third alternative. Rejecting both the indiscriminate baptisms of the kindly old rector who baptized everyone and taught them nothing, and the discriminate baptisms of the rigorist rector who narrowed his teaching task down to his own little flock, and those who had the courage to join them, I propose a third possibility—baptism followed by as much teaching as we can give.

### A Welcoming and Teaching Ministry

When someone with no regular church connection phones me about having a baby "done" I always begin by saying: "I am glad you want your baby to be taught the Christian faith. We would love to do all we can to help you in our church." I explain that Jesus Christ has appointed us to be a school where people of all ages are taught about God, and forgiveness, and life after death. I then ask if they are enthusiastic about giving their child Christian instruction. (For of course, if the child is young, most of the teaching will have to be done by the parents themselves.) Would the parents, or at least one of the parents, be interested in learning about Jesus Christ?

If there is even a spark of interest I immediately schedule a couple of hours in their home with both parents before the baptism to explain the main facts of the Creed: God is the artist of our world, and he wants us to discover what he has in mind. He is more loving than any human parents, and he offers to adopt us into his family. Jesus Christ came from God, went through death, and demonstrated that there is life on the other side. The Holy Spirit of God works in our church to teach us and coach us in the experience of love and joy and peace in our families. I then explain the facilities we have to help the family to learn and grow as Christians.

I always leave a *Good News for Modern Man* New Testament in the home, explain that it is our text book, and show how the family can read a story from the Gospels together, discuss it, and later be able to read to their child. I explain that we can talk to God and tell him just how we feel. I show how we hold a child's hand at bedtime, and express to God the thanksgivings and concerns of the day at the child's own level of language and I urge the family never to ignore a child's spiritual questions. Then I leave my card, explaining that they can call me at any time to ask questions or request prayer. I describe our nursery and Sunday School facilities, and invite the family to worship and to share in our Holy Communion.

Baptisms are in the main service, and, hopefully, church members are friendly and welcoming. Sometimes a member knows the family or lives nearby. I try to get the mother, at least, into a Bible study group for beginners. If members of the congregation can be trained it is good for every new family to have someone to guide them into discipleship and worship.[5] I find that the godparent system very rarely works effectively, and I prefer to leave it as a social formality since it is impossible to ensure that godparents not only belong to our congregation but also know how to do their job.

What then are the results of this approach? I find a few families are very willing to learn, and some, in fact, have asked for baptism for their child because they feel they need a framework of Christian values for their home. A few are obviously hostile. "We just want the child christened, that's all." I do not refuse baptism in such cases, but I insist on giving the family some teaching at least, and make clear that baptism is the entrance into learning from God and that we take this seriously. Most are more or less interested but obviously do not intend to be in church more than is convenient for them. Some of these can later be followed up, and if one has been friendly and warm, they may later welcome further involvement.

## Responsibility Without Rejection

The advantage of this approach is that no family is rejected because the Christian church considers them unworthy, ignorant, or irresponsible. Everybody is welcome, and we are enthusiastic about our school and our teaching. There may be some parents who will avoid baptism for their children because they don't want the embarrassment of refusing to learn. Some will refuse to turn up after registration, but then, every evening school has some who register, pay the course fee, yet fail to attend.

The problem with the afternoon baptisms of the kindly old rector is that the practice gives the impression that something magical is "done" even though no teaching follows. The problem with the young rector, who wants to stop indiscriminate baptism, is that his practice shouts to the world that only well-behaved church members will be taken in. What the practice of the New Testament makes clear is that everyone is welcome, with their families and households. After a brief statement of what the school of Christ has to offer, baptism can be immediate, and since neither Jesus nor his disciples worried about the proportion who might fall away, neither should we!

## A Restriction Because of Distance

What about restrictions due to physical locality? It may
be necessary to say to some potential candidates, "You
live too far away for us to visit you and include you in our
fellowship." This often happens in a missionary situation.
The proper answer should, however, include the encouragement that "We will send you some teachers as soon as
we can, and they will baptize you and start a new school
in your area." The same principle will apply where people
want baptism for themselves or their children in a distant
church for sentimental reasons, like the man who called
me up to say he had been baptized in our church in 1897,
and he wanted his great-granddaughter baptized there. I
explained that I would arrange for a church nearer the
parents' home to enroll and teach the little girl.

The advantage of using the school image in such cases
is that the principle of not enrolling a child from across
the city is well understood in secular terms. I might have
baptized even in such a case if I had felt that I myself,
or someone else, could have driven across and taught the
family in their home, or if it turned out that the family
was obviously willing to bring their child to church from
that distance. As it happened, the man slammed down
the telephone in a huff, but he had admitted and seen the
force of the point that no school would enroll a child unless
there was some way of getting the child to school or the
school to the child. The important principle is that there
is no discrimination because of the lack of qualities in the
child or his parents.

## When Instruction Is Refused

Careful explanation will be required in the case of parents
who want their child baptized but obviously have no intention of learning anything themselves or giving their
child the opportunity of Christian instruction. If the
family lives well outside the reach of the congregation,

the geographical restriction will apply. If, however, they live within visiting reach of the congregation, and there are workers to contact the parents at home and eventually teach the child, it is probably worthwhile registering the child by baptism to make clear that there is no discrimination being practiced as to the parents' character or worth. In such cases it should be made clear at the baptism that the child is now enrolled in the school of Christ, that so-and-so will call to give instruction to the parents about praying for the child, telling Bible stories, and reading and explaining the Bible. If the parents receive the teaching, well and good, especially if they can be encouraged to share in the worship of the church at least occasionally. If, finally, the parents not only refuse instruction at home but prevent their child from being taken to church, the principles still hold and the meaning of baptism is safeguarded. The parents know that they, personally, were not rejected, they can see the meaning of baptism as enrollment in the school of Jesus Christ, they sense the seriousness with which the church cares for its young ones, and any rejection that has taken place is entirely on their part, not the church's.

## What Baptism Is Not

Finally, we make clear by our practice what baptism does not mean. We never suggest that baptism has some magical property in itself. This means that we refuse to encourage hasty baptisms because of imminent death. We also refuse to baptize wherever we have no intention of making efforts to incorporate the candidate into the fullness of the life of the Holy Spirit in the teaching and worshipping church. As we see it, there is no merit in the mere act of enrollment. There must be "the washing of regeneration and the renewal in the Holy Spirit" (Titus 3:5). We accept the fact that in some cases, as in the baptisms in Samaria (Acts 8:4-17), there may be a time lapse between enrollment and the full life of the Spirit. But no baptism should be performed unless there is every intention of making this a reality. We stress again that any discrimination concerns only the church's ability to teach, not the candidates' intentions or worthiness. We demonstrate visibly that no amount of sin, stubbornness, unwillingness, weakness, or faintheartedness, on the part of the pupils or their families, will ever daunt us. It is for such failing, sinning human beings that Jesus Christ came to die. He undertakes to redeem the hardest cases, and the church has the resources of the Holy Spirit to do what would be impossible humanly.

### The Ethiopian Eunuch—an Exception?

We could object that the baptism of the eunuch from Ethiopia violated our principles (Acts 8:26-39). The man in question was moving hundreds of miles away, and there was no incorporation into the fellowship of the Holy Spirit after baptism. The circumstances are, however, exceptional. In the first place, the eunuch was obviously teaching himself by careful study of the Old Testament Scriptures even as he rode in his chariot. It is probable that Philip did intend to teach him more before he was snatched away to do another task. There may already have been some Christians in Ethiopia as a result of what happened on the day of Pentecost. The well-read eunuch had the Scriptures with him, and he understood how Jesus Christ related to them, and so might already have enough understanding of the Good News to begin a new school of the Holy Spirit in his own country. In any case, missionaries would soon arrive there to establish the ancient church in Ethiopia. There are many possibilities, and we do not know the whole story, but one problematical case is not sufficient to shatter the constant New Testament pattern that baptism into the name of Christ is always followed by teaching and fellowship in the school of the Holy Spirit.

## Missions and Mass Baptism

Finally, we apply our school model of baptism to the history of Christian missions. An immediate advantage is that we can make sense of the mass baptisms by which most of Europe was Christianized. Those who insist that genuine faith must precede baptism inevitably view the tribal conversions of Europe as regrettable. The fact is that Europe became Christian as the church took in huge numbers of very raw heathen, and then patiently taught the baptized.

Here are some examples. About AD 300 the whole kingdom of Armenia became Christian under king Tiridates III. In AD 486 King Clovis of the Franks was baptized with three thousand of his soldiers. A hundred years later Augustine and his monks baptized King Ethelbert of Kent and ten thousand of his Saxons. In AD 955 five thousand Magyars of Hungary were baptized and the remainder of the country became Christian, under King Stephen, by AD 1000. Then came Poland under Prince Mieczyslaw and Russia under Emperor Vladimir. King Olave of Norway had most of his country baptized and under instruction by the early eleventh century.[6]

These are the most obvious cases of mass conversion, when a leader of a tribe or nation decided to have his people taught the Christian faith. Admittedly, in certain churches the idea of a probationary period before baptism appeared by the third century. However it would seem that for the first thousand years of church history it was taken for granted in most mission situations that baptism came first and the new disciples were taught later. It would have been inconceivable to start asking each Saxon warrior whether he really believed in Jesus Christ. His reply would have been "My king has ordered it, so I will be baptized with him."

We can say that the work of baptizing most of the nations and tribes of Europe was completed by about

AD 1150.[7] For the next seven centuries virtually no new
nations were added to the Christian churches. By the end
of the nineteenth century, large scale church growth
began again. What is significant is that where this more
recent church growth has been appreciable it can be
demonstrated that baptisms have generally been in large
numbers, without a long probationary period. Admittedly, there have been few cases of a king being baptized
with his tribe, but this is due to the fact that few tribes in
Asia and Africa had a monarch. Where members of a tribe
have become Christians in large numbers, the usual
pattern is a few staunch converts in the beginning. Then
a sub-conscious tribal decision takes place, as the elders
discuss the situation, and weigh up the advantages and
disadvantages of tribal conversion to Christianity. Once
this has taken place, and a positive decision made, the
number of baptisms will be as rapid as the missionaries
permit. The missionaries may think that conversions are
individual and based on genuine faith, but the subsequent
fruits of conversion will depend largely on how well the
arrangements for teaching and worship are provided.

**People Movements and Their Result**
In 1933 Bishop J. W. Pickett of the Methodist Church published his *Christian Mass Movements in India.*[8] Dr.
Donald McGavran called it an "epochal book" which
"marked a turning point in mission History."[9] By carefully surveying some areas where the church has grown
most rapidly, Bishop Pickett was able to demonstrate that
virtually all the growth of the churches in India had been
by mass movements. A mass movement at that time was
defined as a movement which eventually resulted in the
turning of a large proportion of the members of a certain
caste to become Christians.[10]
     Later the term "mass movement" was corrected to
"group movement" or "people movement" as a result of

the huge study of this phenomenon by the world-wide schools of church growth connected with Dr. Donald McGavran.[11] The word "people" is defined, not in racial or national terms, but by identifying them as communities who do not usually marry outside their own grouping. This makes it possible to use one term for a typical early European or modern African tribe, or a caste scattered among many other people over a large part of India, or a clan, or clannish group of people, within a nation or city.

Once Bishop Pickett had drawn attention to the fact of church growth by people movements among certain castes in India, the importance of this type of conversion became obvious. Just as the mass tribal conversions from the tribes of Europe had been despised, in the same way many missionaries and visitors from the sending countries sneered at the very idea of backward peoples being taken into the Christian churches in such large numbers. During the past forty years, more and more instances of people movements have been documented from every continent of the world. Even though Baptist missionaries only baptize adults, yet it has been shown that often their converts have come as a result of a kind of subconscious group decision to become Christians. This is true, for example, among the Naga and other border tribes of India. Most church growth in the African continent has been as a result of taking in large movements from tribe after tribe, and then instructing the converts in worshipping congregations.

This is not the place to describe the vast body of expertise which has been developed to analyze, locate, and encourage the process of church growth by people's movements. My concern is to draw three lessons from this material. A point first made by Bishop Pickett was that it is not the stringency of preparation before baptism that affects the ultimate health of churches, but rather the quality of the teaching and worship after the groups are taken in.

Second, we should note that good or bad motives make very little difference to the outcome. If people come with bad motives, but are well taught after baptism, the results are astonishing. Conversely, if people come with good motives, but the teaching and worship after baptism is poor, the results are depressing. Dr. Warnshuis sums up the results in a few words: "A whole chapter in Dr. J. W. Pickett's thoroughgoing study, *Christian Mass Movements in India,* is given to a critical study of motives, of which forty instances are given. The remarkable conclusion is that the motives which lead people to Christ in people movements are those that lead individuals anywhere to Him. The sick with divers diseases came to Jesus and He healed them. Social, political and economic conditions are not to be wholly separated from religion in Asia and Africa any more than in America and Europe."[12]

Third, there are many examples of people movements being slowed to a standstill by well-meaning missionaries who insist on so much pre-baptismal, individual testing and performance that the social inclination to baptism is killed. Dr. McGavran wrote: "What is done with these first converts is a matter of critical importance. Either the group tendency will be encouraged or discouraged by the preacher. Either he will impose an examination on all members of the group and admit only those who pass the examination as individuals, thus breaking up the natural units and stressing the one-by-one pattern. Or he will count the admission to Christian faith of as large and functional a social unit as possible the more important matter, and will so instruct as to preserve and enhance the social solidarity."[13]

These three sets of empirical facts are provable again and again from the annals of church history and hundreds of missionary case studies. If that is granted it would seem that some form of immediate baptism followed by intensive instruction and worship is the most effective method of encouraging church growth.

## Mixed Motives

Stringent requirements for baptism prevent church growth, and the checking of motives is also proved to be a futile activity. Motives are mostly mixed, and rarely disinterested, even if we assume that being disinterested was a New Testament virtue. If a movement begins among outcasts with the hope of bettering their condition, or among a border tribe for political reasons, who are we to discriminate? We probably began our Christian instruction for equally disreputable reasons: "I liked the singing"; "They were all so friendly"; "My girl friend attended"; "I felt like commiting suicide"; "My husband wanted the kids to go to Sunday School"; "I was forced to go to Sunday School". These and many other motives are as good and bad as each other, but as long as they result in Christian teaching and we accept it, all will be well. If baptism is made the entrance to the church as the school of Christ, and proper arrangements for teaching are provided, we can be as accepting as the New Testament suggests without any fear for the mission of Jesus Christ among the nations.

Earlier in this chapter, my illustrations of the principle underlying a discipleship view of the church used examples of infant baptism. Obviously there has been huge church growth among churches which practice "believers' baptism." The fact that children of baptized adults are dedicated makes no difference to the principle. My argument has been in favor of the immediate baptism of adults. In the New Testament whole households were baptized without any delay (Acts 16:15, 33). We cannot tell from these texts whether the infants in these households were dedicated, or whether they were baptized. The important factor is that church growth is slowed down to a trickle by insistence on rigorous standards of attainment before baptism.[14] I suspect that it could be proved that where Baptist churches have had a typical peoples' movement, most of the baptisms were in fact indiscriminate in the right sense. The missionary may have thought that he was getting a "true" Christian profession, or approved signs of regeneration, but a careful analysis of what actually happened would indicate that the decision to be baptized as a tribe had already been made by the elders and a majority of the families.[15] What made the work effective was the subsequent teaching of the converts and the quality of their worship.

Now the obvious question arises. If it is true that the New Testament churches baptized immediately, and then taught the converts: and if this was the method used to teach and civilize the nations and tribes of Europe, and if it has been the most effective method of church growth in missionary situations in the past century, then surely there must be an application to our task in so-called post-Christian Europe and North America.

## The Western World—A Mission Field

We note that a majority of the people of our western world are no longer Christianized in any effective sense. If they have been baptized as babies, they have never been taught. As children, they have not been to Sunday School, or had any Bible teaching and prayer at home. They have had no experience of regular Christian worship. It is not that they have rejected a genuine Christian way of life. They have never even had the opportunity to discover what it might be. In fact their impression of what is involved is full of misconceptions. To be a Christian is conceived of as a largely negative giving up of good things, living up to impossible standards, swallowing a set of incomprehensible ideas, and then attending some outmoded preaching services. We are therefore back into a typically missionary situation.

Our problem is that we are saddled with a confused image of what we are trying to do. The IBM Corporation used to view itself as a mere maker of business machines. Suddenly it was able to redefine itself in a new way: "We are in the business of processing information." The change affected the mentality of its research scientists, executives, salesmen, and advertising teams, and soon took hold of millions of new customers in business, scientific research, the military forces, and every area of government. The result was huge growth into a vast international corporation which would have been impossible as long as they were thinking only of typewriters and adding machines. At present, most churches suggest that they are in the business of persuading people to be good, believe some abstract doctrines, and come to church instead of enjoying the week-end.

We need to recapture the idea that a Christian is someone who is enrolled to learn about the meaning of our world, to get to know God and all his loving purposes for us in Jesus Christ. The fact is that in every big city, thousands of people are willing to sign up for all sorts of evening courses to become "disciples" of guitar playing, yoga, meditation, marriage encounter, sensitivity training, and much else. It does not occur to the ordinary man that a church is a place to enter and learn. He assumes he would have to say he believed some incomprehensible ideas, measure up to some impossible standards, and dress up with his family every Sunday to appear in church. If he does come to us for baptism the church has habitually checked on his motives, and quickly demanded his time and money to keep the building in repair.

## Two Views of the Problem

The way I picture my task affects every detail of my ministry. One way of looking at the problem is to say: "A hundred years ago the good church members in this parish came to church fifty Sundays in the year, and usually to the evening service as well. All the children of the neighborhood came to Sunday School in the afternoon. Now the average member comes thirty Sundays in the year, and never more than once a Sunday. What if their attendance drops to only twenty Sundays, and then to ten? Can we keep the thing going? How can I get them to be more regular? How do we recruit more attenders?"

With the Discipleship model the problems and the questions are quite different. "What learning opportunities can we offer this fall? Or, if a family is away at their cottage all summer, what books do they need to keep learning? Could we supply them with tapes?" In Ephesus, Paul taught disciples in the hall of Tyrannus (Acts 19:9, 10), so we ask, "What is the best location for teaching new families this year? Should we produce a brochure for the course? Do we advertise on the church page or through the community college?"

As we conclude I hope I have at least demonstrated the fact that the model which we use governs the kind of mission we engage in. From the beginning, Christians have assumed that their job was to teach all nations. They were confident that they could take in new learners by the thousand, and that the Holy Spirit would provide for their Christian education. I reject the mentality that we are in a post-Christian era. The world is wide open to our teaching. All we have to do is to go, make disciples, and teach them all that Jesus Christ has taught us.

**Questions for Study and Discussion**

1   What is done about the baptism, or refusal of baptism, of infants in your church? What impression does it give to parents, to church members, to outsiders?

2   What could be done to improve the teaching of individuals and parents of children who are baptized in your church? Can it all be done by the minister? If not, how can others be trained?

3   If parents insist on baptism for their children, are there ways to refuse without implying that they are not good enough?

4   The author argues that motives are always mixed and motivation irrelevant at the point of baptism. Motives can only be corrected

after teaching by the Holy Spirit. Compare this with the motives of those who enter university, or of children entering primary school. What were your motives when you first came to a church?

5 The church is back into "a typically missionary situation." If you were a missionary sent to propagate Christ's teaching in your area, how would you begin? How do the sects and Hindu cults get a hearing?

## Prayer
*"Thank you, Father, for all those who have had a part in your mission to me. Thank you for parents, friends, teachers. Thank you for books, hospitality, conferences, services to go to any week I choose. Make me part of your loving mission to others."*

## Footnotes
[1] Colin Buchanan suggested that as part of the required discipline, at least one parent should be confirmed and a regular communicant, *Baptismal Discipline,* (Bramcote, Notts.: Grove Books, Grove Booklet No. 3, 2nd. edition, 1974), pp. 17, 21.

[2] "Parents seeking baptism for their child ought to be interviewed, and if necessary instructed, so that a more or less lengthy period of notice ought to be required", *Baptism and Confirmation Today,* (London: S.P.C.K., 1955), p. 2.

[3] There are, of course, many compromises suggested between these two positions. Thus the Report of the Commission on Christian Initiation of the Church of England, *Christian Initiation: Birth and Growth in the Christian Society,* 1971: "the rite of infant baptism may be properly administered to children whose parents show real and positive evidence that initiation into the Church will be accompanied by instruction for life in the faith. We are, indeed, unanimously of the opinion that the Church must never refuse Baptism if sincerely desired for their child by its parents or guardians" (p. 35). A note adds that "a proper criterion of such a sincere desire would be the readiness to receive such preparation as would enable parents to take a sincere part in the public rite of infant Baptism."

[4] Colin Buchanan is so sure that no case for indiscriminate baptism can be made that he writes: "I would disavow any pedobaptist position which relied mainly upon any of: authorities other than Scripture, arguments which would lead to indiscriminate baptism, theologies which make infant baptism different in kind from adult baptism, a devaluation of regeneration, a divorce between baptism and the beginning of the overt Christian life, an automatic efficacy in baptism or a misapplication of the concept of the covenant" (*A Case for Infant Baptism,* 1973, p. 3). By giving some arguments for immediate baptism followed by teaching in the New Testament sense I hope I have met all his other requirements.

[5] This is required in the Diocese of Toronto guidelines for baptism.

[6] See Stephen Neill, *Christian Missions,* Pelican History of the Church, Volume 6, (London: Penguin Books, 1964), pp. 52-117.

[7] Stephen Neill says that the baptism of King Jagiello in 1386, and the subsequent conversion of his Lithuanian people, is usually counted as the end of paganism in Europe. *Christian Missions,* 1964, p. 112.

[8] J. W. Pickett, *Christian Mass Movements in India,* first published in 1933, (Nashville: Abingdon, 1953).

[9] Preface to J. W. Pickett, A. L. Warnshuis, G. H. Singh, & D. A. McGavran, *Church*

*Growth and Group Conversion,* first published in 1936, South Pasadena, Calif.: William Carey Library, 1973), p. vii.

10 Dr. McGavran explains that the term "mass movement" "fails completely to indicate that the movement (a) is not one of mere mass, but always of a people (tribe, caste, or clan); (b) usually enlarges by the conversion of small, well-instructed groups; and (c) achieves large numbers only over a period of years." *Church Growth and Group Conversion,* 1973, p. 4.

11 A full bibliography covering studies from many areas of the Third World is available from The Church Growth Book Club, Box 66, Santa Clara, California 95050.

12 *Church Growth and Group Conversion,* 1973, p. 16.

13 *Ibid.,* 1973, pp. 100, 101.

14 Donald McGavran wrote: "We could safely say that Gathered Church methods have been notably unsuccessful," *How Churches Grow: The New Frontiers of Mission,* first published 1959, (New York: Friendship Press, 1970), p. 23.

15 Dr. McGavran admits as much in the section dealing with gathered churches, *Ibid.,* pp. 20-25.

# Appendix

**The Model Set Out in Propositional Form**

An advantage of a model is that it can be formulated as a set of propositions with its own internal logic. Although no one proposition can be "proved" from the evidence, acceptance of a model includes acceptance of the various implications and results that follow it. In our case the model hangs together around the following propositions, which derive their meaning from the logic of their relationship to one another:

1 John the Baptist used baptism with water to enroll disciples.
2 His disciples grew to large numbers, and included tax collectors, soldiers, and others who had previously been viewed as sinners, or beyond the pale of the Jewish community.
3 As a result of being baptized, the members of the community were viewed as forgiven in the sense of being accepted by the prophet, John, and by one another.
4 John's disciples were taught about a coming kingdom, or community, led by a greater leader in whom the work of the Spirit would be evident.
5 Jesus was baptized by John, and soon after, the Holy Spirit began moving him.
6 Jesus began baptizing his own disciples, among them, some who had been baptized into John's circle of disciples. To move from John's circle of disciples into Jesus' required rebaptism in the name of Jesus.
7 The lifestyle of the disciples of Jesus was radically different from the disciples of John the Baptist. Whereas John and his followers practiced asceticism and lived by the Old Testament law, Jesus' disciples were less concerned about externals.
8 Jesus baptized large numbers, but as illustrated in the parable of the sower, many of these fell away.
9 From among the baptized disciples of Jesus, twelve were chosen as leaders of the community, and these travelled with him on preaching tours.
10 There were other disciples, including some women, who after baptism also followed Jesus more or less closely.
11 In his final instructions, after his death and resurrection, Jesus told the leaders to continue enrolling disciples in his name by baptism, but the world wide growth of the community could only begin after the pouring out of the Spirit in the community.
12 After Pentecost, large numbers of new disciples were enrolled by baptism. Disciples or learners were later called "Christians."

13  Since a disciple was viewed on enrollment as a learner beginning to learn, no probation or tests of spiritual attainment were required before baptism.

14  Men and women, together with dependents such as slaves and children, could be enrolled.

15  However sinful, degraded, or unclean the new disciples had previously been, upon baptism they were immediately viewed as cleansed, or washed from pollution, and their past sins were considered forgiven, no longer to be held against them.

16  The work of Jesus by the Holy Spirit as prophet, healer, anouncer of the kingdom, and teacher continued by the Spirit among the baptized.

17  If, after baptism, the Spirit did not begin his work, apostles came to pray, lay on hands, and organize a community of the Holy Spirit.

18  If the Spirit had already begun his work among a group of unbaptized persons they were baptized immediately.

19  The four characteristic activities encouraged by the Holy Spirit in a new community were: doctrine, fellowship, worship around the bread and wine, and prayer (Acts 2:42).

20  Spiritual gifts such as those of prophecy, teaching, healing, exorcism and speaking in tongues were common among the members of the community. Some of these gifts, such as speaking in tongues, occurred immediately after baptism.

21  As in the Old Testament, false gifts such as those of false prophecy, false teaching, false exorcism, and false glossolalia, abounded among the communities, especially after the departure of apostles.

22  Baptism was therefore no guarantee of spirituality, since many of the baptized committed apostasy, and others became false teachers and prophets in the communities.

23  As the communities spread, there were baptisms first in the area of Jerusalem, then in Judea and Samaria, and eventually throughout the Mediterranean world and to the east. The result was the spreading of the work and teaching of Jesus by the Holy Spirit throughout a vast area.

# Bibliography

The titles, publishers, and dates of publication of books referred to in the text appear in the footnotes at the end of each chapter. The following brief bibliography sets out, according to first dates of publication, highlights of the discussion in its modern form. Only English translations are listed.

*1938*   Emil Brunner forced modern scholars into the debate by questioning the practice of infant baptism.
    *Truth as Encounter.* Philadelphia: Westminster Press, 1964.

*1943*   Karl Barth argued against infant baptism in the Reformed tradition.
    *The Teaching of the Church regarding Baptism.* London: SCM Press, 1948.

*1948*   Oscar Cullmann counterattacked Barth, using the ideas of family solidarity and the argument from circumcision.
    *Baptism in the New Testament.* London: SCM Press, 1950.

*1950*   Pierre Charles Marcel wrote what I take to be the best defense of infant baptism from the Reformed covenant theology viewpoint.
    *The Biblical Doctrine of Infant Baptism.* London: James Clarke & Co., 1953.

*1951*   G. W. H. Lampe successfully began the attack on the Anglican view that baptism had to be completed by confirmation.
    *The Seal of the Spirit,* 2d. ed. London: SPCK, 1967.

*1952*   John Murray used similar arguments to Marcel in *Christian Baptism.* Philadelphia: Orthodox Presbyterian Church, 1952.

*1958*   Joachim Jeremias set out the inscriptional evidence for infant baptism and arguments from Jewish practice.
    *Infant Baptism in the First Four Centuries.* London: SCM Press, 1960.

*1961*   Kurt Aland attacked many of Jeremias' conclusions.
    *Did the Early Church Baptize Infants?* London: SCM Press, 1963.

*1962*   G. R. Beasley-Murray wrote the classic Baptist defense of believers' baptism, but admitted the fact of the strong instrumental nature of the rite.
    *Baptism in the New Testament,* London: Macmillan & Co., 1962.

*1970*   James D. G. Dunn successfully showed the important connection of baptism with the Holy Spirit, but viewed baptism as symbolic, a stimulus to faith.
    *Baptism in the Holy Spirit.* London: SCM Press, 1970.

*1972*   Colin O. Buchanan wrote a small but important statement of infant baptism from the Anglican point of view taking a rigorist view that at least one parent must be a communicant practising Christian.
    *Baptismal Discipline,* rev. ed. Bramcote, Notts.: Grove Books, Booklet No. 3, 1974.

*1973*   Colin O. Buchanan set out *A Case for Infant Baptism,* Grove Books, Booklet No. 20, 1973.

*1974*   David Pawson and Colin Buchanan argued the Baptist response in *Infant Baptism Under Cross-Examination.* Grove Books, Booklet No. 24, 1974.

*1978*   Paul K. Jewett vigorously attacked the Reformed arguments for infant baptism, and gave a very useful bibliography.
    *Infant Baptism and the Covenant of Grace.* Grand Rapids, Michigan: William B. Eerdmans, 1978.

*1978*   Ian Stuchbery set out infant baptism in the context of a parish education program, insights from the charismatic movement, and with much of the feel of new developments in Canada.
    *Growing in Christ: New Patterns of Initiation and Education in the Parish Community.* Toronto: Anglican Book Centre, 1978.

*1979*   Geoffrey W. Bromiley's *Children of Promise: The Case for Baptizing Infants,* Grand
         Rapids, Michigan: Wm. B. Eerdmans Publishing Co., is a much revised and im-
         proved edition of a previous book. The argument is in the same tradition as Gabriel
         Marcel and John Murray (see above).
*1980*   Anthony C. Thiselton's *The Two Horizons: New Testament Hermeneutics and
         Philosophical Description with Special Reference to Heidegger, Bultmann, Gadamer,
         and Wittgenstein.* Grand Rapids, Michigan: William B. Eerdmans Publishing
         Company, 1980, was received too late for inclusion within the text. Thiselton
         documents the hermeneutical revolution that is already affecting New Testament
         studies as a result of Wittgenstein's *Philosophical Investigations,* Oxford: Basil
         Blackwell, 1953 and subsequent editions. My Discipleship model depends on the
         many different meanings of the words "faith" and "believing" (see chapter 5). In
         his book, Thiselton explains the method used, in a section entitled "Polymorphous
         Concepts" (pages 407-427).

# Index of Subjects

# Index of Scripture